ROUTLEDGE LIBRARY EDITIONS: LOGIC

Volume 10

ASPECTS OF A THEORY OF SINGULAR REFERENCE

ASPECTS OF A THEORY OF SINGULAR REFERENCE

Prolegomena to a Dialectical Logic of Singular Terms

WILLIAM J. GREENBERG

Routledge
Taylor & Francis Group

LONDON AND NEW YORK

First published in 1985 by Garland Publishing, Inc.

This edition first published in 2020
by Routledge
2 Park Square, Milton Park, Abingdon, Oxon OX14 4RN

and by Routledge
52 Vanderbilt Avenue, New York, NY 10017

Routledge is an imprint of the Taylor & Francis Group, an informa business

British Library Cataloguing in Publication Data
A catalogue record for this book is available from the British Library

ISBN: 978-0-367-41707-9 (Set)
ISBN: 978-0-367-81582-0 (Set) (ebk)
ISBN: 978-0-367-42024-6 (Volume 10) (hbk)
ISBN: 978-0-367-42616-3 (Volume 10) (pbk)
ISBN: 978-0-367-85400-3 (Volume 10) (ebk)

Publisher's Note
The publisher has gone to great lengths to ensure the quality of this reprint but points out that some imperfections in the original copies may be apparent.

Disclaimer
The publisher has made every effort to trace copyright holders and would welcome correspondence from those they have been unable to trace.

Aspects of a Theory of Singular Reference

Prolegomena to a Dialectical Logic of Singular Terms

William J. Greenberg

Garland Publishing, Inc. ■ New York & London
1985

Library of Congress Cataloging-in-Publication Data

Greenberg, William J. (William Joseph), 1942–
  Aspects of a theory of singular reference.

  (Outstanding dissertations in linguistics)
  Thesis (Ph.D.)—University of California,
Los Angeles, 1982.
  Bibliography: p.
  1. Reference (Philosophy)   2. Semantics (Philosophy)
3. Logic.   4. English language—Categorial grammar.
I. Title.   II. Series.
B105.R25G74   1985   160   85-15897
ISBN 0-8240-5429-6 (alk. paper)

© 1985 by William J. Greenberg

The volumes in this series are printed on
acid-free, 250-year-life paper.

Printed in the United States of America

UNIVERSITY OF CALIFORNIA

Los Angeles

Aspects of a Theory of Singular Reference:

Prolegomena to a Dialectical Logic of Singular Terms

A dissertation submitted in partial satisfaction of the

requirements for the degree Doctor of Philosophy

in Linguistics

by

William Joseph Greenberg

1982

The dissertation of William Joseph Greenberg is approved.

_____
Edward L. Keenan

_____
Robert P. Stockwell

_____
Keith S. Donnellan

_____
Robert S. Kirsner

_____
Paul Schachter, Committee Chair

University of California, Los Angeles

1982

For my Father
and in memory of my Mother

This dissertation has benefited greatly from the detailed comments and criticism of my Chairman, Paul Schachter, and from the encouragement provided by my friend, Saeed Ali. I am grateful to both for helping me through an arduous endeavor.

Aspects of a Theory of Singular Reference:

Prolegomena to a Dialectical Logic of Singular Terms

ABSTRACT OF THE DISSERTATION

Aspects of a Theory of Singular Reference:

Prolegomena to a Dialectical Logic of Singular Terms

by

William Joseph Greenberg

Doctor of Philosophy in Linguistics

University of California, Los Angeles, 1982

Professor Paul Schachter, Chair

The difficulties encountered by attempts to treat identity as a
relation between an object and itself are well-known:

> ...the sentence 'The morning star is...the morning star' is
> analytic and a truism, while...'The morning star is the
> evening star' is synthetic and represents a 'valuable exten-
> sion of our knowledge'... But if [the morning star] and
> [the evening star] are the same object, and identity is taken
> as a relation holding between this object and itself, then
> it is impossible to explain how the two sentences can differ
> in cognitive content... (A. Stroll, "Identity," in The
> Encyclopedia of Philosophy, Vol. 4, p. 123)

Russell's solution to these difficulties rejects the identification of

logical with grammatical form, in effect denying that such sentences

assert relations between the morning (evening) star and itself. The

logical representations which the Russellian proposes, contain quanti-

fiers, predicate letters, and individual variables, but no expressions

standing for particulars. The Fregean solution, while admitting

logical representations whose nominal expressions stand for particulars, insists that the _meaning_ of such expressions is different from their _reference_. Frege-Russell analyses thus both deny that the morning (evening) star is involved qua _particular_ in the meaning of the sentences in question.

Rather than replace the morning (evening) star as ontological subject of these sentences, I suggest that their difference in meaning arises from the _kind_ of particular that the identity-relation relates--a particular which, unlike its Frege-Russell counterpart, is two-sided and multi-faceted. Such a particular requires an ambiguous singular term. In Chapter 1, I utilize such a term to provide a surfacist account of belief-context ambiguity requiring neither differences in relative scope nor distinctions between sense and reference. In Chapter 2, I go on to provide an account of negative existentials, necessity- and identity-statements which _resolves_ philosophical problems that Russell-Frege analyses only _avoid_. To solve these problems, I show that it is necessary to reject two canons of philosophical logic, the Law of Identity and the Indiscernibility of Identicals.

Aspects of a Theory of Singular Reference:

Prolegomena to a Dialectical Logic of Singular Terms

Chapter 1

1.0 The problem[1]

1) Mary's husband is a bachelor.

2) Joan believes that Mary's husband is a bachelor.

3) John's brother is John's brother.

4) Harry doubts that John's brother is John's brother.

Sentences (1) and (3) respectively express a contradiction and a truism. Mary's husband can no more be a bachelor than a square can be a circle; and John's brother's being John's brother is no less certain than John's being John. Yet in belief contexts such sentences appear to take on meanings that they do not ordinarily have. Sentences (2) and (4) are a case in point. As against (1) and (3) (but cf. below), (2) and (4) are ambiguous. In (2), Joan's belief is not necessarily a contradictory one, although it may be. Joan may quite plausibly believe that Henry is a bachelor, in spite of the fact that Henry happens to be Mary's husband. Similarly, in (4), Harry's doubt cannot automatically be dismissed as a product of dementia praecox, although once again it may be. Harry may quite plausibly doubt that Joe is John's brother, although in fact Joe is.

An adequate semantic theory must give a correct account of facts like these. In this chapter I will lay the basis for such a theory. I will propose a logical analysis for sentences like (2) and (4) which explains the nature of the ambiguity in question. The regimented structures that I assign such sentences will correspond to their

1

concrete syntactical structures. The analysis I have in mind attributes the ambiguity present in (2) and (4) to an ambiguity present in all referring expressions ("Mary's husband" and "John's brother" are two such expressions). If my analysis is correct, (1) and (3) are also ambiguous, appearances to the contrary nothwithstanding. I will first try to show that these sentences are ambiguous.

1.1 The singular term: an ambiguous name

"Mary's husband" and "John's brother" belong to that class of expressions which name single entities. Following common philosophical usage, I will call such expressions singular terms. The singular term, I would like to suggest, like other referring expressions functions in all contexts as an ambiguous name. Specifically, I will claim that a singular term ambiguously denotes a particular--an individual object in the actual world--or a property--a form, quality, or relation of a particular. The ambiguity that I am attributing to the singular term entails a logical analysis of (1) and (3) which differs in an important respect from the kind of analysis many philosophers accord such sentences.

Philosophers who construe expressions like "Mary's husband" and "John's brother" as denoting expressions (and there are some who do not), generally agree that in sentences like (1) and (3) such expressions denote particulars if they denote at all. (An example of a non-denoting singular term would be "the present King of France" in a sentence like Russell's "The present King of France is bald". For the moment I will consider only singular terms that denote.) For such philosophers, neither (1) nor (3) is ambiguous. Thus, (1) will assert

2

that the particular denoted by "Mary's husband" <u>has</u> the property denoted by the predicate expression "is a bachelor",[2] while (3) will assert the self-identity of the particular denoted by "John's brother".

The analysis I am proposing, however, provides two distinct interpretations for both (1) and (3). In (1), "Mary's husband" will denote either a <u>property</u> of a particular, MARY'S HUSBAND, or the unique
particular which has that property, Mary's husband. (Upper- and lower-
case spellings will henceforth be used to indicate that an entity is
respectively a property or a particular.) There will therefore be an
interpretation of (1) identical to that mentioned above, on which a
particular, Mary's husband, is attributed the property BACHELOR. On
the second interpretation of (1), however, a particular, Mary's husband,
gives way to a property, MARY'S HUSBAND. What change in meaning does
this shift entail?

To predicate a property of a particular, as in the first interpretation of (1), is to assert that the particular <u>has</u> the property.
In the second interpretation of (1), however, a property is predicated
of a property, not of a particular. But what is it to predicate one
property of another? I will assume here that to predicate property A
of property B is simply to assert that whatever particular <u>has</u> property
B <u>also</u> <u>has</u> property A. Thus, part of what is being asserted on the
second interpretation of (1) is that whatever particular has the property MARY'S HUSBAND also has the property BACHELOR. In other words, part
of what is asserted is that the property MARY'S HUSBAND <u>is</u> <u>included</u> in
the property BACHELOR.

Sentence (3) receives the same kind of analysis as sentence (1).

Just as the predicate expression "is a bachelor" in (1) is taken to denote a property, so "is John's brother" in (3) is taken to denote a property. And just as the singular term "Mary's husband" in (1) is taken to denote ambiguously a particular or a property, so the first occurrence of "John's brother" in (3)[3] is taken to denote one or the other. Thus, on one interpretation, (3) asserts that a particular, John's brother, has the property JOHN'S BROTHER; and on the other, part of what (3) asserts is that a property, JOHN'S BROTHER, is included in the property JOHN'S BROTHER. On this interpretation, (3) also asserts[4] that the property JOHN'S BROTHER is of cardinality one--that is, that one and only one particular has this property. On the corresponding interpretation, (1) likewise asserts that the property MARY'S HUSBAND is of cardinality one.

I would now like to address a question that may be worrying some readers. If sentences like (1) and (3) are ambiguous in the way I claim, why is this ambiguity not apparent? A closer look at the kind of ambiguity involved will, I hope, shed additional light on this matter.

1.20 Logically distinct does not mean logically independent

Although "Mary's husband" in (1) and the first occurrence of "John's brother" in (3) each denote either a particular or a property, the pairs of interpretations I am proposing for each sentence are mutually entailing. I will show that this is so by translating (1) and (3) into English*, a semi-formalized language which, unlike English, has unambiguous singular terms. An English singular term will therefore have two translations in English*, one denoting a particular and the

4

other a property. As a result, the ambiguous English sentence (1) will have two translations in English*, each of which corresponds to one of its interpretations, and similarly for (3). A proof that the pairs of translations in question are mutually entailing--that is, that one is true just in case the other is--will thus also be a proof that the interpretations of the corresponding English sentences are mutually entailing.

1.21 English*

The vocabulary of English* is as presented in (5), and the grammar as in (6). English* glosses of English expressions are given in (7).

5) Vocabulary of English*

(i) Singular terms:

'Mary's husband', 'MARY'S HUSBAND',

'John's brother', 'JOHN'S BROTHER'

(ii) Predicate expressions:

'is a bachelor', 'is John's brother'

6) Grammar of English*

A sentence consists of a singular term followed by a predicate expression.

7) English-English* Equivalents

English	English*
'Mary's husband'	'Mary's husband' 'MARY'S HUSBAND
'John's brother"	'John's brother' 'JOHN'S BROTHER'
'is a bachelor'	'is a bachelor'
'is John's brother'	'is John's brother'

5

The respective English* translations of (1) and (3) are thus (8, 9) and (10, 11).

8)   Mary's husband is a bachelor

9)   MARY'S HUSBAND is a bachelor

10) John's brother is John's brother

11) JOHN'S BROTHER is John's brother

The denotation and truth rules for English* are as follows:

    I.   A predicate expression denotes a <u>property</u>.

    II.   An upper-case singular term denotes a <u>property</u>, and a lower-case singular term denotes a <u>particular</u> if it denotes.

    III.   An upper- and lower-case singular term which translates the <u>same</u> English singular term <u>correspond</u>.

    IV.   If an upper-case singular term denotes a property of cardinality one, the corresponding lower-case singular term denotes the unique particular which has that property; otherwise, the lower-case term does not denote.

12) V.   If a sentence consists of an upper-case singular term followed by a predicate expression, that sentence is true just in case the upper-case term denotes a property of cardinality one which <u>is included</u> in the property denoted by the predicate expression.

    VI.   If a sentence consists of a lower-case singular term followed by a predicate expression, that sentence is true just in case the lower-case term denotes a unique particular which <u>has</u> the property denoted by the predicate expression.

Given (12), it is clear that (8, 9) are mutually entailing. Suppose that (8) is true. Then by (12-VI, I), "Mary's husband" denotes some unique particular $\underline{a}$ and "is a bachelor" some property $\underline{G}$, and $\underline{a}$ has $\underline{G}$. Hence by (12-IV), the corresponding upper-case term "MARY'S HUSBAND" denotes some property $\underline{F}$ of cardinality one, and $\underline{a}$ has $\underline{F}$. Therefore, $\underline{F}$ is included in $\underline{G}$, and so by (12-V), (9) is true. Suppose now that (9)

6

is true. Then by (12-V, I), "is a bachelor" denotes some property G and "MARY'S HUSBAND" some property F, and F is of cardinality one and included in G. Hence by (12-IV), the corresponding lower-case term "Mary's husband" denotes some unique particular a, and a has F. Therefore, a has G, and so by (12-VI), (8) is true. Hence (9) is true if and only if (8) is, and so the two interpretations of (1) are mutually entailing, as are those of (3) and countless other sentences of the same type.

In view of this fact, it is not surprising that sentences like (1) and (3) should not previously have been treated as ambiguous. Attested cases of natural language ambiguity have generally involved classes of sentences with logically independent interpretations not attributable to lexical polysemy. The grounds for treating (1) and (3) as ambiguous are quite different, however. As we will see, the relational objects of belief and doubt are of two sorts: relations of properties and properties, and relations of particulars and properties. But these are precisely the kinds of relations expressed by (1) and (3) under the analysis I am proposing. English* (9) and (11), which correspond to the interpretations of (1) and (3) on which "Mary's husband" and "John's brother" denote properties, assert relations of properties and properties; and English* (8) and (10), which correspond to the interpretations of (1) and (3) on which the expressions in question denote particulars, assert relations of particulars and properties.

As shown above, the kinds of relations in question are mutually necessitating: it could not be otherwise. For a property exists materially only insofar as it is manifest in a particular, and for one

7

property to be included in another, it is both necessary and sufficient that any particular having the one should also have the other. Taken as objects of belief or doubt, however, the verbal reflections of relations of properties and properties, and of particulars and properties, assume an objectively independent character. Our beliefs and doubts can be about properties that we know not which particulars have, or about particulars whose properties are unknown to us. As we will see, this is the objective basis for belief-context ambiguity.

1.3 Belief-context ambiguity

1.31 Singly-embedded belief contexts: an informal account

Let us add to English* the predicate expressions "Joan believes that" and "Harry doubts that". These are expressions that when prefixed to a sentence of English* make a new sentence. We will understand them to have the same meaning as the corresponding expressions in English. Translating (2) and (4) into our informally extended English*, we thus have (13, 14) and (15, 16), respectively.

13) Joan believes that Mary's husband is a bachelor

14) Joan believes that MARY'S HUSBAND is a bachelor

15) Harry doubts that John's brother is John's brother

16) Harry doubts that JOHN'S BROTHER is John's brother

Comparing (13, 14) with (8, 9) and (15, 16) with (10, 11), we notice that one of the things that first puzzled us about belief-context ambiguity, namely, where did it come from, need no longer puzzle us: it was already there. Needless to say, this will be of little consequence unless we can show that the harmless ambiguity postulated for (1) and (3) allows us to provide a correct account of the striking ambiguity present in (2) and (4).

As noted in section 1.0, sentences (2) and (4) each have one implausible and one plausible interpretation. On my analysis, the implausible interpretations correspond to (14) and (16), where the objects of belief and doubt are reflections of relations of properties and properties; and the plausible interpretations to (13) and (15), where the reflections are of relations of particulars and properties. Thus (14) asserts a belief of Joan's that (a) (the property) MARY'S HUSBAND is of cardinality one; and that (b) (the property) MARY'S HUSBAND is included in (the property) BACHELOR. The implausible aspect of Joan's belief is reflected in (b). BACHELORHOOD and HUSBANDHOOD may no more be coexemplified in a particular than CIRCLEHOOD and SQUAREHOOD. The implausibility of the interpretation (16) of sentence (4) has a similar source, although the semantics of doubt is less transparent than that of belief. Thus (16) asserts a <u>belief</u> of Harry's that (a) (the property) JOHN'S BROTHER is of cardinality one; and a <u>doubt</u> of his that (b) (the property) JOHN'S BROTHER is included in (the property) JOHN'S BROTHER. Once again, the implausible aspect of Harry's doubt is reflected in (b).

The implausibility of (14) and (16) stems from the fact that in (14) Joan is attributed a belief in the existence of a particular in which (obviously) incompatible properties co-exist; while in (16) Harry is claimed to doubt whether a property is included in itself. No such hiatus marks (13) and (15), however. With the shift from (the property) MARY'S HUSBAND to (the particular) Mary's husband, and from (the property) JOHN'S BROTHER to (the particular) John's brother, all strangeness disappears: no longer are we faced with a marriage of incompatible properties or a divorce of inseparable ones, but only with mistaken belief and doubt about the relations of a particular and a property.

The following is an informal characterization of the truth rules for sentences like English* (13, 14).

17) Truth Rules

If a sentence consists of "Joan believes that" followed by a sentence consisting of a singular term and a predicate expression, that sentence is true just in case:

a) the singular term is lower-case; and,

    i) the singular term denotes some unique particular $\underline{a}$
    ii) the predicate expression denotes some property $\underline{G}$
    iii) Joan believes that $\underline{a}$ has $\underline{G}$; or,

b) the singular term is upper-case; and,

    i) the singular term denotes some property $\underline{F}$
    ii) the predicate expression denotes some property $\underline{G}$
    iii) Joan believes that $\underline{F}$ is of cardinality one
    iv) Joan believes that $\underline{F}$ is included in $\underline{G}$.

We can now see why the pairs of mutually necessitating relations expressed by (8, 9) and (10,11) can be the objects of entirely independent propositional attitudes. The premise that a property $\underline{F}$ of cardinality one is included in a property $\underline{G}$ licenses an inference that a certain particular $\underline{a}$ in fact has $\underline{G}$ only when supplemented by the premise that $\underline{a}$ has $\underline{F}$. Conversely, the premise that $\underline{a}$ has $\underline{G}$ requires the additional premise that $\underline{a}$ has $\underline{F}$ to license an inference that $\underline{F}$ is included in $\underline{G}$. And so it goes for our beliefs and doubts. A belief (doubt) that $\underline{F}$ is included in $\underline{G}$ is sufficient basis for a belief (doubt) that $\underline{a}$ has $\underline{G}$, and conversely, only when accompanied by the further belief that $\underline{a}$ has $\underline{F}$. Thus Joan may quite plausibly believe, as in (14), that MARY'S HUSBAND is a bachelor, without believing, as in (13), that

Mary's husband is a bachelor, and conversely. Far from being inconsistent, one belief without the other is evidence only for the absence of a further belief that Mary's husband is MARY'S HUSBAND.

A comprehensive account of belief contexts would extend the analysis of this section to sentences in which referring expressions occur in other than subject position:

18) John believes that Harry^i didn't kiss <u>the girl that he^i kissed</u>.

19) John believes that Harry^{i}s car cost <u>more than it^i cost</u>.

I will not dwell upon such sentences, other than to observe that "the girl that he kissed" and "more than it^i cost" in (18-19) are, like "Mary's husband" and "John's brother", ambiguous terms. As a result, the respective objects of "John believes that" in (18, 19):

20) Harry^i didn't kiss <u>the girl that he^i kissed</u>.

21) Harry^{i}s car cost <u>more than it^i cost</u>.

each have a pair of logically distinct but mutually entailing interpretations[6] and make the same contribution to the ambiguity present in (18, 19) as (1) does to that present in (2).

1.32 Multiply-embedded belief contexts

Relying on the notion of an inherently ambiguous singular term, we have been able to show that the <u>de re</u> and <u>de dicto</u> interpretations for (2) flow from the variable reference of the ambiguous term "Mary's husband". The treatment we have proposed for sentences like (2), however, fails to account for the full range of logically independent interpretations typically associated with multiply embedded belief contexts. Sentence (22) is a case in point.

11

22) Edna believes that Joan believes that Mary's husband is a bachelor.

Given our analysis of (2) (cf. English* 13, 14), (22) should have exactly two readings:

23) Edna believes that Joan believes that Mary's husband is a bachelor

24) Edna believes that Joan believes that MARY'S HUSBAND is a bachelor

Our analysis of (2) nothwithstanding, this sentence, like (1), appears to take on, in belief contexts, a meaning that it otherwise lacks. Thus (22) has, in addition to the de re (23) and de dicto (24), a second de dicto interpretation.

Consider. In (24) Edna credits Joan with the belief that a property, MARY'S HUSBAND, is (a) uniquely exemplified, and (b) included in the property BACHELOR. Edna herself takes no stand vis-a-vis the existence of an entity answering to the description "Mary's husband". Yet (22) also has an interpretation according to which Edna believes (a) that the property MARY'S HUSBAND is uniquely exemplified, and (b) that whatever individual in fact has this property is such that Joan believes that individual to be a bachelor. Lacking a source and structure for such a belief, we will, in anticipation of future developments, refer to this reading of (22) as English* (27).

We have been guided so far in our analysis by a principle which I will now make explicit:

25) Given the reference of its parts and their logical arrangement, the meaning of a sentence is fixed.

According to (25), a sentence may have more than one meaning only if it has more than one syntactical analysis or if one of its constituent parts has more than one referent. How then shall we distinguish the two de dicto readings (24) and (27)? Supposing unambiguous reference for English "Edna believes that", "Joan believes that", and "is a bachelor", we have two options. We may, by means of distinct translations for English "Mary's husband" in (24) and (27), attribute ambiguous reference to that term, or we may allow that (24) and (27) have distinct logical arrangements of referentially identical parts. In (24), the term which translates "Mary's husband" denotes the property MARY'S HUSBAND. But MARY'S HUSBAND is just as much an object of belief in (27) as in (24). Hence (27) must, like (24), assign English "Mary's husband" to the category of property-denoting terms, and the difference between the two readings must reside in the logical arrangement of their constituent parts.

In (27) Edna believes that MARY'S HUSBAND is (a) uniquely exemplified, and (b) included in the property any particular has which Joan believes to be a bachelor. To accommodate the structure of the object of Edna's belief, we require a third reading for English (2):

26) (MARY'S HUSBAND)(Joan believes that...is a bachelor)

Taking (26) as the object of English* Edna believes that, we have our second de dicto interpretation for (22):

27) Edna believes that ((MARY'S HUSBAND)(Joan believes
     that...is a bachelor))

In providing this interpretation with a source and structure, we commit ourselves to a fourth reading for both (2) and (22).

28) (Mary's husband)(Joan believes that...is a bachelor)

29) Edna believes that ((Mary's husband)(Joan believes that...
     is a bachelor))

The readings (13, 26, 28) of English (2) are, however, mutually entailing, as are the readings (23, 29) of English (22). To see that this is so, we will extend and generalize the syntactical and semantical rules of English*.

1.321 A categorial grammar for English*

The syntactical rules of English* are of three types. The first type assigns each primitive term and predicate to one of the syntactical categories n, sn, ss. Together with a fourth category s, to which belong certain combinations of primitive terms and predicates, these categories are sufficient for the logical analysis of sentences like English (2, 4, 22).

(i) s: s stands for sentence.

(ii) n: n stands for name.

30) (iii) sn:[7] the category of functors that take an expression of category n as argument and yield as a result an expression of category s.

(iv) ss: the category of functors that take an expression of category s as argument and yield as a result an expression of category s.

The terms "Mary's husband" and "MARY'S HUSBAND" are of the category n, the predicate "...is a bachelor"[8] of the category sn, and the sentence-forming operators upon sentences "Joan believes that" and "Edna believes that" of the category ss.[9]

The second type of syntactical rule, which is recursive, states how syntactical categories combine to form new syntactical categories:

31) Multiplying-Out Rule One

If α is of category ab and β of category b, or α is of category b and β of category ab, then $F_k(\alpha,\beta)$ is of category a.

14

Instances of (31) are (32, 33).

32) If α is of category $\underline{sn}$ and β of category $\underline{n}$, or α is of

category $\underline{n}$ and β of category $\underline{sn}$, then $F_k(\alpha, \beta)$ is of

category $\underline{s}$.

33) If α is of category $\underline{ss}$ and β of category $\underline{s}$, or α is of

category $\underline{s}$ and β of category $\underline{ss}$, then $F_k(\alpha, \beta)$ is of

category $\underline{s}$.

The third type of syntactical rule, also recursive, specifies the
syntactical functions which build up larger expressions from pairs of
smaller ones.

34) If α is of category $\underline{n}$ and β of category $\underline{sn}$, where β is ...Φ,

then $F_1(\alpha, \beta) = \alpha\Phi$.

35) If α is of category $\underline{ss}$ and β of category $\underline{s}$, then

$F_2(\alpha, \beta) = \alpha\beta$.

Given (31-35), we can construct analysis trees for the readings
(13, 14) of English (2). An analysis tree is a graphic representation
of how the syntactical rules of English* operate on pairs of categorized expressions to form new such expressions. For each reading of
English (2), there should be a unique such representation. Thus, given
the strings of categorized expressions:

[Joan believes that]$_{ss}$ [Mary's husband]$_n$ [...is a bachelor]$_{sn}$

[Joan believes that]$_{ss}$ [MARY'S HUSBAND]$_n$ [...is a bachelor]$_{sn}$

and the syntactical rules (31-35), it is possible to construct for
(13-14) the respective analysis trees:

36)

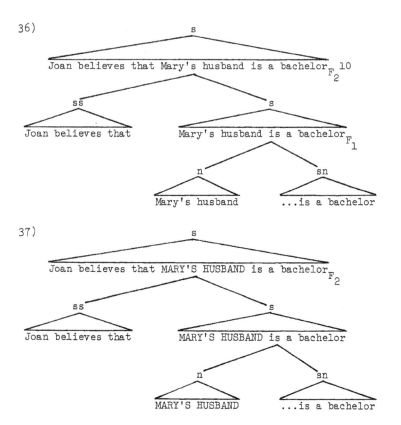

37)

Significantly, however, we have only a partial such representation for
(26), the reading of English (2) which provides a source and structure
for our second de dicto interpretation of (22).

38)

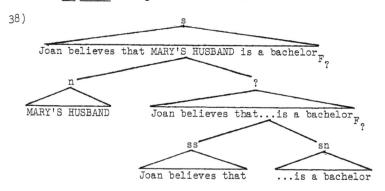

16

To complete (38), we must supplement the multiplying out rule (31) with a multiplying out rule which tells us how an expression of category $\underline{ss}$ combines with an expression of category $\underline{sn}$ to form a new category. We also need to specify the syntactical functions which take "Joan believes that" and "...is a bachelor" into "Joan believes that...is a bachelor", and "MARY'S HUSBAND" and "Joan believes that...is a bachelor" into "Joan believes that MARY'S HUSBAND is a bachelor".

In his important paper "A Program For Syntax,"[11] Geach proposes a multiplying out rule of the appropriate sort. Within our framework, Geach's rule can be stated as:[12]

39) If α is of category $\underline{ab}$ and β of category $\underline{bc}$, then

$F_k(\alpha, \beta)$ is of category $\underline{ac}$.

We thus have, as an instance of (39):

40) If α is of category $\underline{ss}$ and β of category $\underline{sn}$, then

$F_k(\alpha, \beta)$ is of category $\underline{sn}$.

When the $\underline{ss}$ functor "Joan believes that" is applied to the $\underline{sn}$ functor "...is a bachelor", the result, by (40), is an $\underline{sn}$ functor. The syntactical function which amalgamates such expressions can be stated as in (41).

41) If α is of category $\underline{ss}$ and β of category $\underline{sn}$, then

$F_3(\alpha, \beta) = ...\alpha\beta$.

A generalized version of (32) specifies the function which amalgamates an expression of category $\underline{n}$ with an expression, simple or complex, of category $\underline{sn}$.

42) If α is of category $\underline{n}$ and $\gamma\beta$ of category $\underline{sn}$, where β is ...Φ, Φ does not contain "..." and γ is possibly null, then

$F_1(\alpha, \gamma\beta) = \gamma\alpha\Phi$.

17

Rules (39-41) make it possible to replace (38) with the complete analysis tree (43).

43)

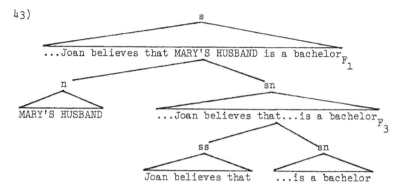

Finally, corresponding to (28), the fourth reading for English (2), we have the analysis tree (44).

44)

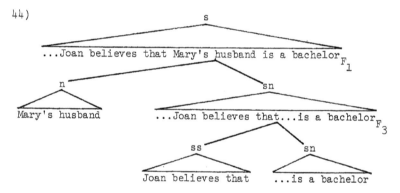

The analysis trees (36, 37, 44, 43) respectively correspond to the labelled bracketings (45, 46, 47, 48). (We will henceforth give all analysis trees as labelled bracketings.)

45) [Joan believes that]$_{ss}$[[Mary's husband]$_n$[...is a bachelor]$_{sn}$]$_s$ [13]

46) [Joan believes that]$_{ss}$[[MARY'S HUSBAND]$_n$[...is a bachelor]$_{sn}$]$_s$

18

47) [Mary's husband]$_n$[...[Joan believes that]$_{ss}$[...is a

bachelor]$_{sn}$]$_{sn}$

48) [MARY'S HUSBAND]$_n$[...[Joan believes that]$_{ss}$[...is a

bachelor]$_{sn}$]$_{sn}$

We will now see that of the four readings for (2), (45, 47, 48) are

mutually entailing.

1.322 The semantics of English*

The denotation rules for English* singular terms and predicate

expressions are as respectively presented in (49, 50), and the truth

rules for English* sentences as presented in (51).

49) Singular Terms

 I. An upper-case singular term denotes a property, and
   a lower-case singular term denotes a particular if
   it denotes.

 II. An upper- and lower-case singular term which
   translate a given English singular term correspond.

 III. If an upper-case singular term denotes a property of
   cardinality one, the corresponding lower-case
   singular term denotes the unique particular which has
   that property; otherwise, it fails to denote.

50) Predicate Expressions

 I. A functor [β]$_{sn}$ denotes a property.

 II. A functor

$$[...[\Phi]_{ss}[[\gamma]_{ss}[...[[\pi]_{ss}[\beta]_{sn}]_{sn}...]_{sn}]_{sn}]_{sn}$$

   denotes a property C such that for all particulars x,
   x has C just in case for some property D, "β"
   denotes D and f(Φ) f(γ) . . . f(π) x has D.

   Conditions:

   i) "f(Φ)", "f(γ)", and "f(π)" are respective English
    translations of the English* functors "Φ", "γ",
    and "π".

   ii) "γ" and "π" are possibly null.

19

51) Truth Rules

I. A sentence

$$[\alpha]_n \, [\beta]_{sn}$$

is true just in case "β" denotes some property $\underline{G}$ such that either:

a) "α" is a lower-case singular term,
b) "α" denotes some unique particular $\underline{a}$, and
c) $\underline{a}$ has $\underline{G}$, or
d) "α" is an upper-case singular term,
e) "α" denotes some property $\underline{F}$,
f) $\underline{F}$ is of cardinality one, and
g) $\underline{F}$ is included in $\underline{G}$.

II. A sentence

$$[\Phi]_{ss}[[\gamma]_{ss}[\, . \, . \, . \, [[\pi]_{ss}[[\alpha]_n[\beta]_{sn}]_s]_s \, . \, . \, . \,]_s]_s$$

is true just in case "β" denotes some property $\underline{G}$ such that either:

a) "α" is a lower-case singular term,
b) "α" denotes some unique particular $\underline{a}$, and
c) $f(\Phi) \, f(\gamma) \, . \, . \, . \, f(\pi) \, \underline{a}$ has $\underline{G}$, or

d) "α" is an upper-case singular term,
e) "α" denotes some property $\underline{F}$,
f) $f(\Phi) \, f(\gamma) \, . \, . \, . \, f(\pi) \, \underline{F}$ is of cardinality one, and
g) $f(\Phi) \, f(\gamma) \, . \, . \, . \, f(\pi) \, \underline{F}$ is included in $\underline{G}$.

Conditions:

i) "$f(\Phi)$", "$f(\gamma)$", and "$f(\pi)$" are the respective English translations of the English* functors "Φ", "γ", and "π".

ii) "γ" and "π" are possibly null.

We will now see that (45, 47, 48) are mutually entailing.

Case (1): Show (47) $\leftrightarrow$ (48)

The proof that (47, 48) are mutually entailing is analogous to that presented in section 1.21 for (8, 9).

20

Case (2): Show (45) ←→ (47)

Suppose that (45) is true. Then, by (51-II), "...is a bachelor" ("β") denotes some property G and "Mary's husband" ("α") some unique particular a, and Joan believes that a has G. Hence for some property D, "...is a bachelor" denotes D and Joan believes that a has D. Therefore, by (50-II), a has the property denoted by the functor:

52) $[...[$Joan believes that$]_{ss} [...$is a bachelor$]_{sn}]_{sn}$

Hence, by (51-I), (47) is true.

Suppose now that (47) is true. Then, by (51-I), the functor (52) denotes some property G and "Mary's husband" some unique particular a, and a has G. Therefore, by (50-II), for some property D, "...is a bachelor" denotes D, and Joan believes that a has D. Hence, by (51-II), (45) is true.

We see, then, that the readings (45, 47, 48) are mutually entailing. As a result, the four readings for English (2) fall into two equivalence classes of logically independent readings: (45, 47, 48) and (46).

Returning to English (22), we find that, given the two multiplying out rules (31) and (39), this sentence has more readings than we had bargained for. Thus, as an instance of (39), not only do we have rule (40), we also have rule (53).

53) If α is of category $\underline{ss}$ and β of category $\underline{ss}$, then $F_k(α, β)$ is of category $\underline{ss}$.

The syntactic function which combines two $\underline{ss}$ functors and produces a new $\underline{ss}$ functor is specified in (54).

54) If α is of category $\underline{ss}$ and β is of category $\underline{ss}$, then $F_4(α, β) = α$.

(53) and (54) take the ss functors "Edna believes that" and "Joan believes that" into the new ss functor "Edna believes that Joan believes that". The latter can in turn combine with the sn functor "... is a bachelor" to yield, by (40) and (41), the sn functor:

55) $[...[[$Edna believes that$]_{ss}[$Joan believes that$]_{ss}]_{ss}$
$[...$is a bachelor$]_{sn}]_{sn}$

Thus, corresponding to each of the following strings of categorized expressions:

56) $[$Edna believes that$]_{ss}[$Joan believes that$]_{ss}[$Mary's husband$]_n$
$[...$is a bachelor$]_{sn}$

57) $[$Edna believes that$]_{ss}[$Joan believes that$]_{ss}[$MARY'S HUSBAND$]_n$
$[...$is a bachelor$]_{sn}$

there are five logically distinct readings for (22), which thus has ten readings in English*:

58) $[$Edna believes that$]_{ss}[[$Joan believes that$]_{ss}$
$[[$Mary's husband$]_n[...$is a bachelor$]_{sn}]_s]_s$

59) $[$Edna believes that$]_{ss}[[$Joan believes that$]_{ss}$
$[[$MARY'S HUSBAND$]_n[...$is a bachelor$]_{sn}]_s]_s$

60) $[$Edna believes that$]_{ss}[[$Mary's husband$]_n$
$[...[$Joan believes that$]_{ss}[...$is a bachelor$]_{sn}]_{sn}]_s$

61) $[$Edna believes that$]_{ss}[[$MARY'S HUSBAND$]_n$
$[...[$Joan believes that$]_{ss}[...$is a bachelor$]_{sn}]_{sn}]_s$

62) $[$Mary's husband$]_n[...[$Edna believes that$]_{ss}$
$[...[$Joan believes that$]_{ss}[...$is a bachelor$]_{sn}]_{sn}]_{sn}$

63) $[$MARY'S HUSBAND$]_n[...[$Edna believes that$]_{ss}$
$[...[$Joan believes that$]_{ss}[...$is a bachelor$]_{sn}]_{sn}]_{sn}$

64) [[Edna believes that]$_{ss}$[Joan believes that]$_{ss}$]$_{ss}$
[[Mary's husband]$_n$[...is a bachelor]$_{sn}$]$_s$

65) [[Edna believes that]$_{ss}$[Joan believes that]$_{ss}$]$_{ss}$
[[MARY'S HUSBAND]$_n$[...is a bachelor]$_{sn}$]$_s$

66) [Mary's husband]$_n$[...[[Edna believes that]$_{ss}$
[Joan believes that]$_{ss}$]$_{ss}$[...is a bachelor]$_{sn}$]$_{sn}$

67) [MARY'S HUSBAND]$_n$[...[[Edna believes that]$_{ss}$
[Joan believes that]$_{ss}$]$_{ss}$[...is a bachelor]$_{sn}$]$_{sn}$

We will now see that these ten readings fall into three equivalence classes of logically independent readings: (58, 60, 62, 63, 64, 66, 67), (59, 65), and (61).

1.323 Logically distinct does not mean logically independent

Case (1): Show (66) $\leftrightarrow$ (67)

This proof is analogous to that presented in section 1.21 for (8, 9).

Case (2): Show (62) $\leftrightarrow$ (63)

This proof is analogous to that presented in section 1.21 for (8, 9).

Case (3): Show (58) $\leftrightarrow$ (64)

Suppose that (58) is true, and let "Φ", "γ", "π", "α", and "β" in (51-II) respectively be "Edna believes that", null, "Joan believes that", "Mary's husband", and "...is a bachelor". Then, by (51-II), "...is a bachelor" denotes some property $\underline{G}$ and "Mary's husband" some unique particular $\underline{a}$, and Edna believes that Joan believes that $\underline{a}$ has $\underline{G}$. Now let "Φ" be the complex $\underline{ss}$ functor "Edna believes that Joan believes that", "π" be null, and "γ", "α", and "β" be as before. According to

(51-II), a sentence with such a structural analysis is true just in case "...is a bachelor" denotes some property G and "Mary's husband" some unique particular a, and Edna believes that Joan believes that a has G. Sentence (64) has such a structural analysis, and so (64) is true.

Proof of the converse is left to the reader.

Case (4): Show (58) ⟵⟶ (62)

Suppose that (58) is true, and let "Φ", "γ", "π", "α", and "β" in (51-II) respectively be "Edna believes that", null, "Joan believes that", "Mary's husband", and "...is a bachelor". Then, by (51-II), "...is a bachelor" denotes some property G and "Mary's husband" some unique particular a, and Edna believes that Joan believes that a has G. Hence, for some property D, "...is a bachelor" denotes D and Edna believes that Joan believes that a has D. Now let "Φ", "γ", "π", "α", and "β" in (50-II) assume the same values that they assumed in (51-II). We accordingly have that the functor

68) [...[Edna believes that]_{ss}[...[Joan believes that]_{ss}
         [...is a bachelor]_{sn}]_{sn}]_{sn}

denotes, by (50-II), a property C such that for all particulars x, x has C just in case for some property D, "...is a bachelor" denotes D and Edna believes that Joan believes that x has D. Hence a has C, and so by (51-I), (62) is true.

Suppose now that (62) is true, and let "α" and "β" in (51-I) respectively be "Mary's husband" and the complex sn functor (68). Then, by (51-I), "Mary's husband" denotes some unique particular a and the sn functor (68) some property G, and a has G. Now let "Φ", "γ", "π", and "β" in (50-II) assume their values of the last paragraph. As a result, we have that $\underline{G} = \underline{C}$. Hence, for some property $\underline{D}$, "...is a bachelor" denotes $\underline{D}$ and Edna believes that Joan believes that $\underline{a}$ has $\underline{D}$. Now let "α" in (51-II) be "Mary's husband" and "Φ", "γ", "π", and "β" be as above. We therefore have, by (51-II), that (58) is true.

Case (5): Show (60) ↔ (62)

Suppose that (60) is true, and let "Φ", "γ", "π", "α", and "β" in (51-II) respectively be "Edna believes that", null, null, "Mary's husband", and the $\underline{sn}$ functor:

69) [...[Joan believes that]$_{ss}$[...is a bachelor]$_{sn}$]$_{sn}$

Then, by (51-II), "Mary's husband" denotes some unique particular $\underline{a}$ and the functor (69) some property $\underline{G}$, and Edna believes that $\underline{a}$ has $\underline{G}$. Hence, for some property $\underline{D}$, (69) denotes $\underline{D}$ and Edna believes that $\underline{a}$ has $\underline{D}$. Now let "Φ", "γ", "π", and "β" in (50-II) be as above. The $\underline{sn}$ functor (68) thus denotes a property $\underline{C}$ such that for all particulars $\underline{x}$, $\underline{x}$ has $\underline{C}$ just in case for some property $\underline{D}$, (69) denotes $\underline{D}$ and Edna believes that $\underline{x}$ has $\underline{D}$. The particular $\underline{a}$ thus has $\underline{C}$, and hence, by (51-I), (62) is true.

Suppose now that (62) is true, and let "α" and "β" in (51-I) respectively be "Mary's husband" and the $\underline{sn}$ functor (68). Then, by (51-I), "Mary's husband" denotes some unique particular $\underline{a}$ and (68) some property $\underline{G}$, and $\underline{a}$ has $\underline{G}$. Now let "Φ", "γ", "π", and "β" in (50-II) respectively be "Edna believes that", null, null, and the complex $\underline{sn}$ functor (69). (68) thus denotes the property $\underline{C}$ and $\underline{G} = \underline{C}$. Hence, by (50-II), for some property $\underline{D}$, (69) denotes $\underline{D}$ and Edna believes that $\underline{a}$ has $\underline{D}$. Letting "α" in (51-II) be "Mary's husband" and

"Φ", "γ", "π", and "β" be as above, we thus have that (60) is true.

Case (6): Show (64) ⟷ (66)

The proof of case (6) is analogous to that of case (4).

Case (7): Show (59) ⟷ (65)

The proof of case (7) is analogous to that of case (3).

It follows from cases (1-6) that (58, 60, 62, 63, 64, 66, 67) are mutually entailing, and from case (7) that (59, 65) are mutually entailing. The ten readings for English (22) thus fall into three equivalence classes: (58, 60, 62, 63, 64, 66, 67), (59, 65), and (61). Each class consists of pairwise mutually entailing readings, and all of the readings belonging to any one class are logically independent of the readings belonging to the other two classes.

1.4 Conclusion

In summary so far: we see that there is a fundamental ambiguity in the English singular term; that singular terms commonly held to denote particulars denote properties of particulars as well; and that sentences like (1) have, as a result, pairs of logically distinct but mutually entailing readings which give rise to logically independent de dicto and de re interpretations for sentences like (2). We also see in (2) different logical arrangements of referentially identical parts, resulting in logically distinct but mutually entailing readings which give rise, in multiply iterated belief contexts such as (22), to pairs of logically independent de dicto interpretations.

It should be remarked that the preceding characterization of belief-context ambiguity rests on a theory of singular reference whose correctness will turn on its ability to solve a number of other reference-related problems which have received a great deal of attention from philosophers in this century, and which have increasingly exercised linguists concerned with the study of meaning. Three such problems arise in connection with the logical analysis of singular sentences about existence, identity and necessity. We will see in Chapter Two that a theory of singular reference based on the one proposed here can provide solutions for these problems as well.

1. This chapter has benefited throughout from Edward Keenan's helpful suggestions and criticism.

2. The predicate expression "is a bachelor" is itself analyzable. The analyzability of such expressions is not, however, germane to the issue at hand. For the sake of simplicity, such expressions will in chapters one and two, be treated as unitary.

3. The second occurrence of "John's brother" in (3) likewise ambiguously denotes a particular or a property. As noted above, however, predicate expressions like "is John's brother" are being treated as unanalyzable.

4. The truth-conditions for such sentences are presented in section 1.21.

5. Words bearing identical superscripts are to be understood as having the same reference.

6. This is an over-simplification. Suppose that Harry's car cost $800. Then (19) will be true of (A) John believes that Harry's car cost, e.g., $900, or if (B) John has no fixed amount in mind, but believes that Harry's car cost more than $800, or if (C) John, implausibly, believes that whatever Harry's car cost, it cost more than that. In (A), the object of John's belief is a relation of a particular sum of money and a property, and in (B) and (C) the objects of his beliefs are relations of properties and properties. Hence, in (A), John believes that the sum of money denoted by the (complex) term "cost more than (what) it[1] cost" has the property denoted by the predicate expression "Harry[1]s car cost..."; in (B) that the property MORE THAN $800 is included in the property denoted by "Harry[1]s car cost..."; and in (C) that the property MORE THAN (WHAT) IT[1] COST is included in the property in question. An analysis of (21) along the lines I have proposed would yield three logically distinct but mutually entailing interpretations which would give rise to the three logically independent interpretations indicated for (21).

7. This notation is due to Geach.

8. The notation "..." will henceforth be used to mark the argument place for expressions of the category sn.

9. The functor "Joan believes that" may be analyzed as consisting of a predicate expression "Joan believes", which takes a that-clause to make a sentence, and the functor "that", which takes a sentence to make a that-clause. The simplification here effected treats "Joan believes that" as unanalyzable.

10. The functions F_i in analysis trees are those specified in (34, 35).

11. Cf. Geach (1970), pp. 239-40.

12. Op. cit., p. 240.

13. In replacing analysis trees with labelled bracketings, I leave out of account the syntactical functions F_1 - F_4. The labelled bracketings make explicit only the categorial structure of the readings they represent.

Chapter Two

In this chapter, the following philosophically problematic sentences have been selected for analysis.

1) Pegasus does not exist.

2) Scott is the author of Waverley.

3) Necessarily, the number of planets is odd.

First, the problems posed by such sentences for the traditional subject-predicate logic are canvassed, and Russell and Frege's correctives to that tradition discussed in comparative detail. Stock is then taken of the semantical and metaphysical views which give rise to the strictures which Russell places upon the notion of a logically proper name. These views are found to have a common source: Russell's concept of the kind of particular that such a name must name.

For the particular that Russell posits, unlike the qualitatively definite objects and events of everyday life, is a bare particular, a that but not a what, an existence but not a content, a phantom entity separate from and prior to its determinations. Russell's concept of the particular thus restricts itself to the individual, which Russell sets over against the universal as an independent and self-subsistent entity, and identifies with the particular itself.[1]

The tension between the object and its concept brings forth a series of dilemmas. For the concept is inadequate to reflect the existence or non-existence of its object, the nature of its identity or non-identity with other objects, or the fact that it has some of its

30

characters essentially and others nonessentially. But Russell does not attribute these dilemmas to the failure of his concept to capture both sides of its object. He attributes them instead to a failure of the traditional subject-predicate logic to separate and counterpose particular and general propositions, as he separates and counterposes, in his notion of the particular, the individual and the universal. Russell thus sets out to make the logic of the object correspond to the logic of his concept. The instrument of this endeavour is the ontologically "perfect" calculus of _Principia Mathematica_. Here pride of place goes to the _logically proper_ name, a singular term which, as his concept of the particular, is separate from and counterposed to its predicates.

The burden of this chapter is thus threefold. First, I will show that the difficulties Russell raises for a subject-predicate logic of singular terms are inseparably linked, via a "no-sense" theory of proper names, to a conception of the particular as an entity divorced from its characters. Then, I will show that the _qualitatively definite_ particular of everyday life requires a singular term _and_ a proper name which, unlike Russell's "logically proper" name, embrace _both_ of its aspects, its thatness _and_ its whatness, the individual _and_ the universal. The singular expressions I have in mind may thus refer to a property of a particular, a _fragment_ of its whatness, a _universal,_ or to the _ground_ of that whatness, an _individual_. Finally, I will show that taken together with the _kind_ of particular they signify, such singular expressions provide the basis for an ontological solution to the problems which arise in the attempt to understand the logic of singular statements about existence, identity, necessity and belief. This solution will in turn be seen to make possible a theory of logical form for English singular sentences which involves neither a Russellian distinction between grammatical and logical form nor a Fregean bifurcation of sense and reference.

The pre-modern mode of logical analysis which Russell and Frege called into question treated logical and grammatical form as coinciding at the level of survace structure. Thus associated with the pre-modern mode was an intuitive and naive theory of logical form whose linguistic basis was the subject-predicate structure of simple declarative sentences in many languages. Because the grammatical subject and predicate of (e.g.) "Socrates is mortal" are "Socrates" and "is mortal", the pre-modern mode also treated these as the logical subject and predicate of the corresponding proposition. On what might thus be termed the surfacist approach of the pre-modern tradition, such philosophically problematic statements as (1-3) were also taken to be logically of the subject-predicate form.

In addition to a reliance on grammatical as an index to logical form, the pre-modern mode was also characterized by a reference theory of meaning and a correspondence theory of truth. According to the former, a logically significant word or phrase signified an extra-linguistic entity, and it was this entity which constituted its meaning. In the pre-modern tradition, the meaning of "Socrates" was thus the individual Socrates, and that of "is mortal" the property mortality; and the sense of "Socrates is mortal" was that Socrates exemplified mortality. Just as the reference theory of meaning had recourse to the real world for the meanings of logical subjects and predicates, so the correspondence theory of truth also established the real world as the locus of propositional truth and falsity: a proposition was to count as true if the _designata_ of its logical parts were related as proposed, and as false otherwise. Thus, the truth of "Socrates is mortal" reflected the fact that in the real world, Socrates exemplified mortality.

For a central core of simple, subject-predicate sentences, the surfacist approach of the pre-modern tradition yielded analyses which were compatible with a reference theory of meaning and a correspondence theory of truth. It was thus possible to treat "Socrates" as the logical subject of "Socrates is mortal" without doing violence to the notion of a reference theory of meaning. For it could be plausibly maintained that one unfamiliar with the meaning of "Socrates" could be suitably instructed by being introduced to Socrates himself. To treat "Socrates is mortal" as a subject-predicate proposition was, moreover, ontologically circumspect. For the truth of such a proposition presupposed a universe populated with nothing more extravagant than particulars and their properties.

But the surfacist approach came into conflict with its two companion doctrines where the logical analysis of other subject-predicate structures was concerned. Particularly troublesome was the analysis of statements about, or at least apparently about existence and identity, and the analysis of the propositional objects of necessity and belief. Instructive in this regard is the dilemma associated with the often-cited negative existential

1) Pegasus does not exist.

Suppose "Pegasus" to be a constituent of the proposition expressed by (1). (A word or phrase will be a constituent of a proposition if it stands for—or could stand for—an object whose properties or relations ground the truth or falsity of the proposition in question.) Then either "Pegasus" stands for an object, or it does not. Suppose that it does. Then the sense of (1) will be that this object lacks a property, existence. Therefore, either (1) is only apparently true, or "Pegasus" stands for a non-existent object. Suppose, on the other hand, that "Pegasus" does not stand for an object. It would then seem that (1), despite its apparent truth, must account as asserting nothing at all. For an assertion must be an assertion about something.

We are thus caught on the horns of a dilemma. The truth of (1) presupposes a universe peopled with non-existent objects. But, to avoid such a universe, we must discount (1) as either false or meaningless. Nor is the affirmative "Pegasus exists" any less problematic. Once more, unless we concede a universe peopled with non-existent objects, we must account "Pegasus exists" as true if "Pegasus" stands for an object, or as meaningless if it does not. Thus are we unable to reflect the non-existence of Pegasus.[2]

Singular statements which apparently involved the identity-relation posed problems of a different sort. Thus, suppose that "Scott" and "the author of Waverley" are constituents of the proposition expressed by (2);

2) Scott is the author of Waverley.
and that "is" in (2) is the "is" of identity. The sense of (2) is then that Scott and the author of Waverley are numerically identical.

Now if Scott or the author of Waverley do not exist, (2) will have to count as asserting nothing, since "Scott" and "the author of Waverley" are by hypothesis constituents of (2), and a meaningful proposition must be about something. Yet the meaningfulness of (2) does not seem to depend on the existence of either Scott or the author of Waverley. On the other hand, if these individuals do exist, (2) will have to constitute a necessary truth, since by hypothesis the "is" of (2) is the "is" of identity. For according to Leibniz, when two individuals are one and the same, they must have the same properties, and hence the same essential properties. Therefore, since identity-with-Scott is an essential property of Scott, if the author of Waverley and Scott are numerically identical, identity-with-Scott must also be an essential property of the author of Waverley . Yet the identity of Scott and the author of Waverley, unlike the self-identity of Scott, would certainly appear to be a contingent one.

Necessity statements provided a third source of difficulty for the pre-modern mode. Thus, consider the following triad:

4) Necessarily, nine is odd.

5) Nine is the number of planets.

3) Necessarily, the number of planets is odd.

Suppose that "nine" and "the number of planets" are logical constituents of (3-5), and that "is" in (5) is the "is" of identity. (4), (5) and (3) will thus respectively assert the essential oddness of nine, the numerical identity of nine and the number of planets, and the essential oddness of the number of planets. Now nine is essentially odd, and the identity of nine and the number of planets is a matter of astronomical follow from (4) and (5). Yet (3) is false,[3] although (4) and (5) are true. Nine could not be nine if it were not also odd, yet the number of planets could, e.g. change from nine to eight while still continuing to be the number of planets.

A series of problems thus hindered pre-modern attempts to assess the logical role of singular terms, especially as these occurred in statements which, at least apparently, attributed (non)existence or identity to things or necessity to their relations. Russell and Frege attributed these problems to different sources. For Russell, such problems resulted from the pre-modern identification of logical with grammatical form. Russell thus called into question the presumption that English singular terms (including what are ordinarily called "proper names") are _logical_ constituents of the propositions in whose verbal expressions they stand.

To solve these problems, Russell transforms statements such as (1-3) into logically equivalent statements in which singular terms nowhere occur as constituents. For Russell, the propositional content of (1-3) is thus given by syntactically reconstructed formulae which contain no grammatically significant expressions that refer to particulars. Russell's solution thus rejects the presumption that (1-3) are about the particulars to which their singular terms ostensibly refer. Frege's solution, on the other hand, while preserving an essentially surfacist approach to the logic of singular terms, also rejects the presumption that (1-3) are about the objects they appear to be about. Thus according to Frege, a singular term, in addition to (sometimes) having a reference, also expresses a _sense_, and it is the sense of a singular term rather than its reference which is involved in the meaning of (1-3). Thus, whereas for Russell the propositional content of (1-3) is given by _syntactically_ reconstructed formulae that contain no expressions which refer to particulars, for Frege their propositional content is given by _semantically_ reconstructed formulae, in which such terms are replaced by terms which refer to _senses_. Russell and Frege thus both retreat from the position which I will here advocate: that the immediate ontological and epistemological subject of (1-3), and of singular sentences generally, is the _particular_.

My position thus entails the rejection of a Fregean separation of sense and reference, according to which not the reference but the _sense_ of a singular term is involved in the propositions expressed by (1-3).[4] For if a particular is the ontological subject of (1-3), then reference _to_ the particular is necessary to determine the content thereof, and the character of our knowledge of that content. My position also entails the rejection of a Russellian distinction between grammatical and logical form for singular sentences. For such a distinction, when consistently carried out for singular terms (as in Quine '60), makes direct reference to particulars impossible. Finally, and most importantly, my position entails a rejection of the _kind_ of particular which gave rise to the brand of syntactical and semantical reconstructionism practised by Russell and Frege: a particular which precludes such distinctions as existence and non-existence, identity and difference, and essence and accident. The goal of Russell's syntactical and Frege's semantical reconstructionism was to _avoid_ the paradoxes which such a particular placed in the way of attempts to explain the meaning of statements about existence, identity and necessity. They accomplished their goal by eliminating, or replacing the particular as ontological and epistemological subject. My goal here is to resolve such paradoxes. For this I require a particular which admits these crucial distinctions. Logic has suffered long enough the tyranny of a particular whose nature excludes them.

The retreat from the particular as ontological and epistemological subject finds its most consistent syntactical expression in Russell's doctrine of the singular term as an incomplete symbol. W. Kent Wilson explains what it is for a symbol to be incomplete, in Russell's sense:

> A symbol s is an incomplete symbol in a sentence when (i) s occurs as a phrase which is classified as grammatical subject or object according to the (superficial) grammar of that language; (ii) the result of a correct analysis (a logical grammar) yields a sentence which contains no grammatically [or semantically] significant expression corresponding to s.[5]

The reconstruction of:

6) The author of Waverley is mortal.

according to the eliminative technique developed by Russell in Principia Mathematica, yields a three-part statement which contains no grammatically or semantically significant expression corresponding to "the author of Waverley":

    i.   Something authored Waverley.

7)   ii.   Not more than one thing authored Waverley.

    iii. Whatever authored Waverley is mortal.

In symbolic terms, the reconstruction of the subject-predicate proposition

8) $M(_1xAWx)$,

where "$_1xAWx$" is a value of an individual variable, yields a propositional function which contains instead the predicate expression "AW",
a value of a predicate variable:

9) $Vx(AWx . \Lambda y(AWy \leftrightarrow y=x)) . \Lambda z(AWz \rightarrow Mz)$

When put into what according to Russell is their proper logical form,
(6, 8) are thus seen to lack a singular term as logical subject. Correspondingly, we will now see, they come to lack a particular as
ontological subject, and indeed to lack an ontological subject at all.

The elimination of the ontological subject of (6, 8) takes place
in two steps. First, the attribute of uniquely having authored
Waverley is extruded from the particular it is an attribute of, and
made to do duty for the particular itself. This step corresponds to
the replacement of a particular-denoting expression by one which expresses an attribute, as in:

10) the author of Waverley $\longrightarrow$ THE AUTHOR OF WAVERLEY,

or symbolically, as in:

11) $_1xAWx \dashrightarrow {}_1XAWX$[6]

Here, capital letters signify the reconstruction of a particular as an
attribute. The second stage of this replacement we can represent as:

12) THE AUTHOR OF WAVERLEY $\dashrightarrow$ authored Waverley,

or as in:

13) $_1XAWX \dashrightarrow AW$

Here, a uniquely exemplifiable attribute is separated from the specifi-
cation of its cardinality, and changed from a subject to a predicate.
Postponing until 2.4 a presentation of the third and final stage in the

reconstruction of <6, 8> as <7, 9>, let us focus upon the semantical ramifications of an ontological metamorphosis not yet wholly in view.

According to Russell's brand of paraphrasis, (7) and (9) are not about particulars, as their unreconstructed counterparts appear to be. Hence they are not _particular_ propositions. Instead they are _general_ propositions--general in that if they were about anything, they would not be about particulars but attributes of particulars. They are, however, not about attributes of particulars; lacking a logical subject, they also lack an ontological subject, and so are not _about_ anything.[7] Russell's retreat from the particular as ontological subject, as realized in his elimination of the singular term as logical subject, thus gives rise to an analysis according to which: (A) singular sentences convey not particular but general propositions; and, (B) general propositions lack logical subjects.

The line of reasoning in terms of which Russell attempts to establish (A) and (B) presupposes a parallelism of structure between proposition and fact. Two semantical doctrines determine the nature of this relation: the reference theory of meaning and the picture theory of language. I will discuss these doctrines and the relation they determine in _2.0_, _2.1_ and _2.2_. In _2.3_, I will employ this relation to show that (B) rests upon an incorrect account of the structure of general facts. I will then argue that a correct account of this structure requires that an attribute be allowed to function as an _ontological_ subject, and so also that an attribute-expression such as "THE AUTHOR OF _WAVERLEY_" in (12) and "$_1$XAWX" in (13) be allowed to function as a _logical_ subject. The stage corresponding to (12, 13) in the Russellian elimination of the particular as ontological subject will therefore be judged to be incorrect.

2.0 The reference theory of meaning

The meaning of a name is what it refers to. This is the nerve of the reference theory of meaning. Russell subscribes to a strong form of this theory in his early treatise The Principles of Mathematics (hereafter PM), where he treats all words as names. In Chapter IV of PM he asserts: "Words all have meaning, in the simple sense that they are symbols that stand for something other than themselves."[8] The meaningfulness of a word--and each word is, for the Russell of PM, in this sense meaningful--thus resides in its connection with some sort of extra-linguistic entity.

In PM Russell recognizes two sorts of names, proper and general. Proper names include proper nouns like "John", de-adjectival and de-verbal nouns like "humanity" and "death", and complex expressions like "every man", "some man", and "all men", as well as phrases of the form "a so-and-so" and "the so-and-so". General names include common nouns like "dog", adjectives like "human", verbs like "die", and complex expressions like "King of England". Each name stands for, or indicates an extra-linguistic entity, which is its meaning. A general name indicates a concept, a universal[9] with which we are acquainted. Proper names indicate things or concepts: the simple proper name "John" indicates a thing, while the complex proper names "every man", "some man", and "the present King of France", derived from the general names "man" and "present King of France" by the addition of "every", "some" and "the", indicate concepts.

The meaning of a sentence is, for the Russell of PM, a proposition, an extra-linguistic entity which contains not words but the entities indicated by words, that is, things and concepts. Any thing or concept which occurs in a proposition as a logical subject--as that about which the proposition asserts something--Russell calls a term of a proposition.

On the basis of the notion term of a proposition, Russell distinguishes two sorts of proper names. "Socrates" indicates a thing and "humanity" a concept which, since they function as logical subjects in the propositions expressed by "Socrates is human" and "Humanity belongs to Socrates", are terms of these propositions. Unlike such proper names, however, proper names of the form "a so-and-so" and "the so-and-so", along with other what Russell is later to call denoting phrases, indicate concepts which cannot function as logical subjects.[10] Such concepts, according to Russell, themselves denote things, and it is the things so denoted rather than the concepts which denote them that propositions are about, and which hence occur as terms in propositions.[11] In Russell's words:

> A concept denotes when, if it occurs in a proposition, the proposition is not about the concept, but about a term connected in a certain peculiar way with the concept. If I say "I met a man", the proposition is not about a man; this is a concept which does not walk the streets, but lives in the shadowy limbo of the logic-books. What I met was a thing, not a concept, an actual man with a tailor--and a bank-account or a public-house and a drunken wife.[12]

As with "a so-and-so", so with "the so-and-so":

> The word the, in the singular, is correctly employed only in relation to a class-concept of which there is only one instance. We speak of the King, the Prime Minister, and so on...: and in such cases there is a method of denoting one single definite term by means of such a concept..."[13]

42

Just as the concept indicated by "a man" is not a term of the proposition expressed by "I met a man", the proposition being instead about a thing denoted by this concept, so the concept indicated by, e.g. "the author of Waverley" is not a term of the proposition expressed by "the author of Waverley is mortal", which instead is about Scott, the single definite thing denoted by that concept.[14]

In his controversial piece "On Denoting" (1905) (hereafter OD), Russell abandons the PM thesis that the meaningfulness of any word, and by implication, any grammatically significant group of words, resides in its connection with some extra-linguistic entity. Thus in OD "the author of Waverley", which in PM Russell would have treated as a complex proper name, is no longer a name but a denoting phrase. Unlike a name, which "has a meaning by itself, without the need of any context,"[15] a denoting phrase "does not...have any significance on its own account."[16] In his introduction to the second edition of PM (1937), Russell criticizes the PM view that such expressions are names:

> This way of understanding language turned out to be mistaken.
> That a word 'must have some meaning'...is not always true if
> taken as applying to the word in isolation. What is true is
> that the word contributes to the meaning of the sentence in
> which it occurs: but that is a very different matter.[17]

The strong version of the reference theory of meaning expounded in PM has thus been replaced by a weaker version: some words and groups of words, among which in particular denoting phrases like "a man" and "the author of Waverley" are not names but incomplete symbols, which "have absolutely no meaning whatsoever in isolation but merely acquire a meaning in context."[18]

The proposition itself undergoes a change in ontological status during the years 1903-1919, although in none of his writings does Russell achieve a consistent account of what a proposition is. In PM, a proposition is the meaning of a sentence, and like a thing or concept, part of the ultimate furniture of the universe. In OD, the status of the proposition is somewhat less certain: although it contains the entities which words indicate, denoting phrases sometimes occur in the proposition (rather than in its verbal expression); and the proposition, like other linguistic entities, now has a meaning. In "The Philosophy of Logical Atomism" (1918-19) (hereafter PLA), the proposition is no longer an extra-linguistic entity but "just a symbol...a complex symbol in the sense that it has parts that are also symbols."[19] Yet like its PM progenitor, the PLA proposition continues to have parts which belong to the extra-linguistic world: "...the constituents of propositions... are the same as the constituents of the corresponding facts."[20] Whether its constituents, or indeed the proposition itself is regarded as symbol or object, in Russell's post-PM logical analysis, denoting phrases and other "incomplete symbols" never stand for genuine constituents of a proposition. In PM, it will be recalled, grammatically correct denoting phrases like "a man" or "the author of Waverley" were treated as complex proper names standing, albeit indirectly, for the things which the concepts that they indicated denoted. In OD and Russell's subsequent work, howevever, such expressions are instead treated as incomplete symbols, and the things which in PM they had in some sense referred to, cease to be constituents of the propositions in which such phrases occur. In PLA Russell expresses this point in the following way:

..when I say 'The author of Waverley is human', "the author of Waverley" is not the subject of that proposition, in the sort of way that Scott would be if I said 'Scott is human', using "Scott" as a name... 'The author of Waverley is human'...does not contain a constituent "the author of Waverley".[21]

A little later, discussing the difference between denoting phrases and names, Russell says:

> You think that the proposition 'Scott is mortal' and the proposition 'The author of Waverley is mortal' are of the same form. You think that they are both simple propositions attributing a predicate to a subject. That is an entire delusion: one of them is (or rather might be) and one of them is not. These things, like "the author of Waverley", which I call incomplete symbols, are things that have absolutely no meaning whatsoever in isolation but merely acquire a meaning in context. "Scott" taken as a name has a meaning all by itself. It stands for a certain person, and there it is. But "the author of Waverley" is not a name, and does not all by itself mean anything at all, because when rightly used in propositions, these propositions do not contain any constituent corresponding to it." (emphasis added)[22]

Therefore, although Russell states in OD that a phrase is a denoting phrase by virtue of its grammatical form alone, it is propositional form which he invokes as ultimate ground for the judgment that such phrases are not names but incomplete symbols: a denoting phrase is an incomplete symbol and not a name because in whatever proposition such a phrase may occur, as in, e.g. "The author of Waverley is mortal" or "I met a man", there is no constituent corresponding to that phrase as a whole, which in the "true analysis" of the proposition breaks up and disappears.

If, however, grammatical form is not a reliable guide to propositional form, on the basis of what is propositional form to be established? More to the point, what backing has Russell for the claim that unlike "Scott" in "Scott is mortal", "the author of Waverley" is not a logical constituent of "The author of Waverley is mortal"?

45

Finally, if the latter of these propositions is not of the subject-predicate form, then what structure _does_ it have, and what entities does it contain as constituents?

To come to grips with questions such as the aforegoing, we will now consider what influence was had upon Russell's analysis of propositional form by the philosophy of logical atomism, a metaphysical doctrine of which, during the years 1914-22, Russell and Wittgenstein were the two leading exponents. Two important and characteristic features of Russell's logical atomism will concern us here--the picture theory of language and Russell's inventory of the different kinds of facts in the world. For these doctrines together provide a metaphysical rationale for the logical distinctness of proper name and denoting phrase, and so constitute the extra-logical basis of Russell's contention that singular terms such as "the author of _Waverley_" are not constituents of the propositions in whose verbal expression they occur.

2.1 The picture theory of language

Borrowed from the German mathematician Heinrich Hertz by Wittgenstein and elevated to philosophical pre-eminence in the _Tractatus Logico-Philosophicus_, the picture theory of language provides Russell with the connecting link between the form of a proposition and the form of a fact. The central thesis of the picturing doctrine is that between a proposition and a stste of affairs which it asserts to exist, there is an _identity_ _of_ _structure_ in virtue of which a true sentence "pictures" the fact that it describes.

By his own accounting, Russell was much influenced by Wittgenstein's picturing doctrine, which had its genesis in pre-_Tractatus_

46

writings that Wittgenstein had given Russell in 1914. Although Russell nowhere presents a connected account of a picture theory of language, a version of the doctrine he must have held can be put together on the basis of passages from a number of his writings.

To begin with, for Russell as for Wittgenstein, a fact is something _complex_, an entity which has _parts_ with _relations_ between them:

> When things are complex, they consist of parts with relations between them. A table consists of legs and a flat top. A knife consists of a handle and a blade. Facts...consist always of relations between parts of a whole or qualities of single things.[23]

How its parts are interrelated constitutes the _form_ of a fact. This form remains constant when the constituents of the fact are changed. Therefore, two facts:

> ...have the same 'form' when they differ only as regards their constituents. In this case, we may suppose the one to result from the other by _substitution_ of different constituents. For example, 'Napoleon hates Wellington' results from 'Socrates loves Plato' by substituting Napoleon for Socrates, Wellington for Plato, and hates for loves. It is obvious that some, but not all, facts can be thus derived from 'Socrates loves Plato'. Thus some facts have the same form as this, and some have not. We can represent the form of a fact by the use of variables: thus 'xRy' may be used to represent the form of the fact that Socrates loves Plato.[24]

It is this form which, according to Russell's picturing doctrine, the correct symbol for a fact, a sentence or proposition, must reproduce:

> ...in a logically correct symbolism there will always be a certain fundamental identity of structure between a fact and a symbol for it.[25]

A proposition which shared the structure of the fact it symbolized was a pictorially adequate proposition, and it was just such propositions that the analysis of denoting phrases as incomplete symbols was meant to produce.

The thrust of the picturing doctrine is thus that the complexity of a proposition is not _sui generis_, but mirrors instead the complexity of an extra-linguistic entity, the fact that the proposition, if true, would symbolize. So Russell's contention that "Scott" in "Scott is mortal" is (or might be) a proper name, while "the author of _Waverley_" in "The author of _Waverley_ is mortal" is not, presupposes a certain analysis of the corresponding facts: given the picture theory of language, the form of a proposition is parasitic upon the form of a fact. Thus Russell's claim that "Scott" is (or might be) a constituent of "Scott is mortal", while to "the author of _Waverley_" there corresponds no constituent of "The author of _Waverley_ is mortal", ultimately comes to rest upon facts about facts.

A complete account of the world, according to Russell, requires more than an enumeration of the particular things that are in it. It also requires an account of the relations of these things, and of their properties, all of which are _facts_.

> The things in the world have various properties, and stand in various relations to each other. That they have these properties and relations are _facts_, and the things and their qualities or relations are quite clearly in some sense or other components of the facts that have those qualities or relations.[26]

Among the types of facts which Russell distinguishes, we will confine our attention to those most pertinent to his analysis of propositional form, the _particular_ and the _general_.

2.2 Particular facts

A particular fact consists in the possession of a quality or relation by some particular thing(s):

> When I speak of a 'fact'...I mean that a certain thing has
> a certain quality, or that certain things have a certain
> relation.[27]

The simplest such fact connects a particular and a quality (which

Russell identifies with a monadic relation), as in, e.g. "This is

white"; the next simplest, two particulars and a binary relation, as in,

e.g. "This is to the left of that", and so on. Together Russell refers

to these as <u>atomic</u> facts. The constituents of an atomic fact are a

monadic or "...dyadic or triadic or tetradic...relation," and "...be-

sides the relation, the terms of the relation--one term if it is a

monadic relation, two if it is dyadic, and so on."[28] A <u>term of a rela-</u>

<u>tion</u> in an atomic fact--conceptually comparable to the term of the <u>PM</u>

proposition--must, unlike its <u>PM</u> progenitor, which could be either a

particular <u>or</u> a concept--belong to the category of <u>particulars</u>.

An <u>atomic</u> proposition is correspondingly one which "...asserts

that a certain thing has a certain quality, or that certain things have

a certain relation",[29] and so asserts an atomic fact. In such a propo-

sition, a constituent expressing a monadic relation (or quality) is,

according to Russell, a "predicate", and one expressing a higher-order

relation a "verb". A constituent standing for a <u>term</u> of a relation is

a <u>logical</u> <u>subject</u>. Now since Russell admits only particulars as terms

of relations, a logical subject can only be a constituent standing for

a particular. Russell holds, moreover, that "proper names = words for

particulars." A logical subject, therefore, can only be a word for a

particular, a <u>proper</u> <u>name</u>.

To particular facts and propositions, which have particulars and

particular-words as constituents, and have subject-predicate form,

Russell opposes general facts and propositions, which do not have particulars or particular-words as constituents, and lack subject-predicate form. This separation and counterposition of particular and general facts paves the way for the elimination of the singular term as logical subject. For if "The author of <u>Waverley</u> is mortal" corresponds not to a particular but a general fact, then in view of the picturing doctrine, ample ontological warrant exists for the claim that "the author of <u>Waverley</u>" is not a logical subject, as "Scott" is (or might be) in "Scott is mortal".

2.3 <u>General facts</u>

In view of the special role of facts and their forms in determining the correct analysis of monadic singular sentences, one would expect Russell to provide for general facts a treatment comparable in depth and detail to that which he provides for particular facts. Russell provides nothing of the sort, however, for beyond the bare assertion that a general fact "...is about all or some of a collection,"[30] Russell has nothing to say about the analysis of general facts, which, he avers, is "...an exceedingly difficult question, and one which I should very much like to see studied."[31] However, an indication of the lines along which such a treatment might proceed comes from Susan Stebbing, who in her book <u>An Introduction to Modern Logic</u> (1930) suggests a structure for general facts quite like that which Russell proposes for <u>particular</u> facts.

What Stebbing suggests is that "general propositions are directly about properties which individual objects may possess"[32] rather than the objects (if any) which possess these properties. Thus, in the proposition "All squares are rectangles", what is asserted is not a relation between a particular (or particulars) and a property, as in, e.g. the particular proposition "This is a rectangle", but a "connection between two properties or characteristics" such that if "anything has the property of being a square, it also has the property of being a rectangle."[33] The fundamental difference between a particular and a general fact would thus appear to be that in the latter, a term of a relation is a universal--or to use Russell's terminology, a concept-- rather than a particular. But if this is so, particular and general facts differ essentially in the kinds of things they connect, and not otherwise.

Thus, returning to Russell's account of the form of a fact, it is clear that once a term of a relation in a general fact is accounted a universal, the claim that particular and general facts differ fundamentally in point of form is without warrant. For, as Russell points out, two facts "...have the same 'form' when they differ only as regards their constituents."[34] Surely then, to borrow one of Russell's examples, if the property of being a man functions as a term of a relation in the general fact that all men are mortal, this fact will result from the particular fact that Socrates is mortal through the substitution of a property, that of being a man, for the particular Socrates. Hence if we assume for facts, as Russell does for propositions, that their form is "that which is in common between any two... of which the one can be obtained from the other by substituting other constituents for the original ones",[35] particular and general facts with the same number of constituents will share a common form.[36]

Russell, nevertheless, treats particular and general facts and propositions as totally dissimilar in form. Thus, in My Philosophical Development (1959), Russell credits Peano with a "technical advance" which hastened the downfall of the traditional Aristotelian logic, and which represented a logical reform of some importance for the philosophy of mathematics. The advance in question: Peano's separation of propositions of the form 'Socrates is mortal' from those of the form 'All Greeks are mortal', which according to Russell, "in Aristotle and in the accepted doctrine of the syllogism are treated as indistinguishable, or, at any rate, as not differing in any important way."[37] In fact, however, Russell misrepresents the Aristotelian position, and so obscures the fundamental issue at hand. So far from treating such propositions as "indistinguishable" or "as not differing in any important way," the traditional logicians held that the distinction between such propositions was "primarily a metaphysical distinction, viz., that the 'singular subject' was a substance, whereas the subject of the A proposition ["All Greeks are mortal"] was not,"[38] in effect referring their logical difference to the content, and not the form, of the corresponding facts. Had Russell followed the example of the traditional logicians, the development of modern logic might very well have taken a different course: this is beyond my competence to judge. What is indubitable, however, is that if n-adic general facts differ from n-adic particular facts not in respect of their form, but in respect of the category of things which function as terms, then propositions which "picture" monadic particular and monadic general facts must share the same form. Russell can deny to such facts a common form, however, for as noted earlier, he holds that only a _particular_ may function as a term of a relation.[39]   It remains to examine the warrant for such a contention.   But first a clarification.

Although Russell in _PLA_ conceives of a proposition as "just a symbol," in practise he employs "subject", "predicate", and "verb"-- locutions which are most often understood as referring to words or phrases--interchangeably with "term of a relation", "attribute", and "relation", locutions which refer to constituents of facts.   Many critics have seen in Russell's haphazard deployment of such terms a failure to distinguish between use and mention.   However, another construction may plausibly be placed upon his use of these terms in the passages we are about to examine.   In _PM_, it will be recalled, Russell treats the proposition as an _extra-linguistic_ entity whose constituents are not symbols but things and concepts.   Such a conception naturally lends itself to an identification of the constituents of a proposition with the constituents of facts, and thence to a conflation of the terms which refer to each type of constituent.   Indeed, just such a levelling is apparent in Russell's remarks on particulars and relations, where he asserts, for example, that a particular occurs only as the "subject" of a proposition.   Literally construed, such an assertion involves a confusion of use with mention.   For if propositions, and their constituents, are conceived as symbols, then particular-_words_, but not particulars _themselves_ may function as their subjects.   On the other hand, if the constituents of propositions are conceived as _extra_-linguistic entities, as in _PM_, then Russell's conflation of the constituents of propositions with the constituents of facts loses its paradoxical cast: a particular

53

may then, without prejudice, be treated as both the subject of a proposition and a term of a relation in a corresponding fact. In presenting Russell's remarks on the privileges of occurrence of particulars and relations, we will thus have recourse to the PM notion of a proposition. We will so accomplish two things. First we will avoid placing upon Russell's discussion an unfavorable construction for which there is little textual support; and second, we will be able to pass directly from Russell's strictures on the occurrence of attributes and relations in propositions to the corresponding strictures on their occurrence in facts.

Russell endows particulars on the one hand, and attributes and relations on the other, with markedly different privileges of occurrence. Thus, a particular, quite in the manner of an Aristotelian first substance, "never occurs in a proposition except as the subject or as one of the terms of a relation."[40] In contract, "a relation can never occur except as a relation, never as a subject."[41] For unlike a particular, which "stands entirely alone and is completely self-subsistent,"[42] attributes and relations "suggest a structure," so that "all propositions in which an attribute or a relation seems to be the subject are only significant if they can be brought into a form in which the attribute is attributed or the relation relates."[43]

To shed some light on the preceding, we will first consider the nature of the distinctions particular/attribute and term-of-a-relation/attribute. We will then be able to bring Russell's remarks about particulars and attributes into a more perspicuous form.

Particular and _attribute_ designate ontological _types_: to be a particular or an attribute is to belong to one of two ontological kinds, which in their various combinations and interconnections make up much of the ultimate furniture of the universe. _Term of a relation_, on the other hand, designates an ontological _function_: to be a term of a relation is simply to be connected in a certain way with a relation or attribute inside the context of an atomic fact. The contrasts particular/attribute and term-of-a-relation/attribute are therefore of quite a different order. Nothing may be both a particular and an attribute, for these categories represent mutually exclusive (but inextricably interconnected) aspects of things. But whether something may be both an attribute and a term of a relation is an entirely different question. For what kind of entity may function in a given way inside an atomic fact depends wholly upon the kinds of entities there are in the world and upon their respective characters and interrelations; and these are surely not matters to be decided on by stipulation, as Russell attempts to do in _PLA_, where he simply lays it down that "particulars = terms of relations in atomic facts."[44] As Veatch observes, Russell's statement, if true, represents not a fact about the word "particular" or even about Russell's concept of a particular, but rather a fact about the particular itself.[45] Accordingly, it is the real world, and not a philosopher's fiat, which must deliver up the distribution of particulars and attributes in atomic facts.

The basis for Russell's refusal to allow an attribute to function as a term of a relation is his notion of a particular as "complete" in a sense that an attribute is not. Thus, while a particular "stands

alone and is entirely self-subsistent," an attribute, according to
Russell, is incomplete: unlike a particular it "suggests a structure",
of which any fact into which it enters must bear the imprint. So a
fact in which an attribute _seems_ to function as a term of a relation
must instead be analyzed as one in which the entity in question functions as a verb or predicate.

But just what _is_ this "suggestion of a structure", this "incompleteness" present in an attribute but not in a particular, in virtue
of which each must fulfill a separate function in an atomic fact? For
a particular is surely no more capable than an attribute of standing,
"alone and entirely self-subsistent": particulars can no more exist
apart from their attributes, than attributes can exist apart from the
particulars which exemplify them. Thus, inasmuch as a member of either
ontological category can exist just in case it is connected with a member (or members) of the other, the incompleteness of an attribute in no
way distinguishes it from a particular. Russell can thus not invoke
the incompleteness of an attribute to justify the privileged occurrence
of a particular as a term of a relation in an atomic fact. The thesis
that only a particular may function in this way thus rests upon a distinction without a difference. In rejecting this distinction, and
therewith Russell's stricture on the occurrence of attributes as terms
of relations in atomic facts, we so remove the metaphysical warrant
for denying general propositions subject-predicate form. Contrary to
Russell, then, the transformation of an attribute-word from logical
subject to predicate, as in (12) and (13),

    (12)   THE AUTHOR OF <u>WAVERLEY</u> --> authored <u>Waverley</u>

13) $_1$XAW --→ AW

and the corresponding reconstruction, as a propositional function, of a

general proposition that we can now represent as

14) THE AUTHOR OF WAVERLEY is mortal,

or symbolically as

15)   M($_1$XAWX)

cannot be made to repose upon facts about facts.

2.4 General propositions and propositional functions

In this section, I will take up three main points: (i) the

nature of the relation I assert to hold between the subject and predi-

cate of a monadic general proposition; (ii) the nature of the relation

between such a proposition and the propositional function which Russell

takes to express its logical form; and, (iii) the nature of the entity

which an individual variable in such a propositional function can assume

as a value.

(i): The relation involved in a monadic general proposition is

one which holds between attributes A and B whenever having A entails

having B. Fitch calls this relation inclusion, for "it is the relation

of one attribute to another if the former is 'included' in the latter."[46]

Inclusion is thus involved in both (14) and (15), in (14) as expressed

by the word "is", and in (15) by the device of juxtaposition of subject

and predicate.

Now, inclusion is the characteristic mode of connection of attri-

butes, as contrasted with exemplification, which is the characteristic

mode of connection of particulars and attributes. Accordingly, "is"

signifies the inclusion relation in general propositions, and the exemplification relation in particular propositions. The copula should not therefore be treated as an ambiguous sign, as Fitch and many others hold it to be. Instead, inclusion and exemplification should be treated as modifications of a self-same identity-relation, induced by terms differing among themselves in ontologically pertinent ways.[47]

(ii): The relation between a general proposition, and a propositional function which Russell takes to embody its logical form, is that of <u>ground</u> to <u>consequent</u>. Thus, consider the universal proposition

    16) ALL MEN are mortal,[48]

and its Russellian transcription

    17) $\Lambda x(MAN(x) \dashrightarrow MORTAL(x))$.

The truth of (16) consists in its correspondence to a general fact constituted by the inclusion of the attribute of being a man in the attribute of being mortal. But, attributes exist only in, and through their connection with the things that have them. Therefore, the inclusion of MAN in MORTAL realizes itself in the fact that <u>men</u> are mortal. And from <u>that</u> fact follows the truth of (17).

The elimination of the denoting phrase as logical subject has already been seen to involve the reconstruction of a general proposition as a propositional function. One aspect of that reconstruction was seen to involve (cf. p. 39) the removal of an attribute from subject to predicate position. A further aspect reveals itself in the replacement of (16) by (17): the reduction of the <u>inclusion</u> relation to a class of <u>exemplification</u> relations. The connection between <u>being</u> a man and <u>being</u> mortal thus amounts, according to Russell's brand of paraphrasis, to nothing more than a (possibly infinite) class of <u>unrelated</u> <u>particular</u> <u>facts</u>:

58

18) $(MAN(x_1) . MORTAL(x_1)) . (MAN(x_2) . MORTAL(x_2)) \ldots$
$(MAN(x_n) . MORTAL(X_n))$

For the only possible relation between such particular facts would reside in their connection with the **general** fact that the attribute MAN
is included in the attribute MORTAL. Yet, the reconstruction of (16)
as (17), **reduces** that general fact to the class of particular facts
which only that fact can **explain**. The replacement of (16) by (17) thus
constitutes the reduction of a ground to its consequent.

(iii): The particulars over which Russell's individual variables
range are **bare** **particulars**. To understand what a bare particular is,
it will help to consider the ancillary notions **external** **property** and
necessarily external **property**.

A property f will be understood as **external** to a particular just
in case f is not essential to the particular—that is, just in case the
particular could remain what it is, even if it lacked f:

19) $EXT(f, x) \longleftrightarrow Pos(x=x . \sim f(x))$

Having two legs is thus external to a mathematician but not to a
cyclist, for a mathematician could remain a mathematician after losing
a leg, but a cyclist could not, in similar circumstances, remain a
cyclist.

A property f will be understood as **necessarily** **external** to a
particular just in case f is not essential to what the particular is,
and furthermore, the particular is what it is **necessarily**:

20) $Nec(EXT(f, x)) \longleftrightarrow Pos(x=x . \sim f(x)) . Nec(x=x)$

Having two legs is thus external to a mathematician, but it is not
necessarily external, for a mathematician is a mathematician only
contingently.

Accordingly, a particular will be necessarily such that all properties are external to it, just in case no property is essential to it, and furthermore, it is what it is necessarily:

21) Nec Λf(EXT(f, x)) $\longleftrightarrow$ Pos Λf(x=x . ~f(x)) . Nec(x=x)

A particular which is <u>necessarily</u> such that <u>all</u> properties are external to it is what shall be meant by the phrase "bare particular":

22) BP(x) $\longleftrightarrow$ Nec Λf(EXT(f, x))

Moreover, if a particular is what it is <u>necessarily</u>, then every property can be external to it just in case it is not possible for any property to be internal[49] to it:

23) Nec(x=x) $\longrightarrow$ [Pos Λf(x=x . ~f(x)) $\longleftrightarrow$

~Pos Vf(Nec(x=x $\longrightarrow$ f(x)))][50]

From (21, 22, 23) it follows that a particular is bare just in case: (i) it is not possible for there to be a property which is internal to it; and, (ii) the particular is what it is necessarily:

24) BP(x) $\longleftrightarrow$ ~Pos Vf(Nec(x=x $\longrightarrow$ f(x))) . Nec(x=x)

Thus, precisely because it is <u>necessarily</u> what it is, a bare particular can have no <u>other</u> property necessarily:

25) BP(x) $\longrightarrow$ ~Pos Vf(Nec(f(x)))[51]

From (24), however, it also follows that a particular which is <u>not</u> bare is a particular which can either have an internal property, or not be what it is necessarily, or both:

26) ~BP(x) $\longleftrightarrow$ Pos Vf(Nec(x=x $\longrightarrow$ f(x))) v ~Nec(x=x)

Suppose that <u>a</u> is not a bare particular, but is necessarily self-identical. Then from (26) we have

27) Pos Vf(Nec(f(a))).

We will now see why a cannot belong to the domain of Russell's individual variables.

Russell's conception of the particular is akin to the old conception of substance. According to this conception, substance is something which is logically simple, its simplicity residing in the fact that it depends on nothing other than itself for the logical possibility of its existence.[52] A bare particular is simple in this sense; lacking the potential for necessary properties, it depends for its existence only upon itself. It is in this sense that for Russell a particular must be logically simple. But a is not simple in this sense. For the non-bareness of a consists in its potential for necessary properties, and hence for depending upon something other than itself for the possibility of its existence. It is this logical complexity which debars a from the value range of Russell's individual variables.

To sum up so far: Russell's elimination of the singular term has been shown to involve two semantical theses: (A) singular sentences convey not particular but general propositions; and, (B) general propositions, unlike particular propositions, lack logical subjects. Given Russell's picturing doctrine, we have seen that (B) rests on an ontological thesis: (B') general facts, unlike particular facts, lack ontological subjects. (B') has in turn been shown to depend on the doctrine that attributes, unlike particulars, are "incomplete". Thus, according to Russell, while a particular can function as a term of a relation in a particular fact, an attribute cannot function in this way in a general fact. For, an attribute, unlike a particular, "suggests a structure", and so presumably cannot fill one. Rather than provide a general fact with an ontological subject, Russell does away with the fact altogether. He accomplishes this by recasting as predicates, attributes which appear to function as terms, while replacing inclusion and other relations between attributes by classes of exemplification relations between particulars and attributes. A general fact is thus abolished in favor of the class of particular facts to which it gives rise: a consequence becomes its own ground. Lest such a class of particular facts itself send forth an attribute as a term of a relation, moreover, the particular becomes, in Russell's hands, a bare particular whose intrinsic nature is innocent of attributes. As a term of a relation in a purely particular fact, Russell requires an entity whose nature is not to have a nature.

The reduction of general facts to classes of particular facts corresponds, in Russell's logical analysis, to the reconstruction of general propositions as propositional functions. In this reconstruction, attribute-words are separated from specifications of their generality, and moved from subject to predicate. Individual variables are then designated to mark the positions of particulars in the resulting classes of particular facts, and appropriate combinations of quantifiers and connectives to represent the relations of such classes. Such a process culminates in the reconstruction of (28) as (7)

28) THE AUTHOR OF WAVERLEY is mortal

    i. Something authored Waverley.

7) ii. Not more than one thing authored Waverley.

    iii. Whatever authored Waverley is mortal.

--and of (29) as (9).

29) $M(_1 XAWX)$

9) $Vx(AWx \cdot Ay(AWy \longrightarrow y=x) \cdot Az(AWz \longrightarrow Mz))$

But such a reconstruction rests upon an incorrect account of general facts. For the "incompleteness" of an attribute in no way distinguishes it from a particular, and thus fails to justify a structural difference between general facts and particular ones. There is thus no ontological warrant for the supposition that an attribute can function only as a predicate, and hence that general propositions lack subject-predicate form.

At this point, it might be tempting to object that ontological considerations aside, the problems surrounding the logic of statements about existence, identity and necessity provide sufficient warrant for denying to sentences (1-3) a subject-predicate form. To meet this objection, I will propose an analysis for the sentences in question.

2.5 The puzzles

2.51 Existence statements

Unlike mortality and honesty, which are properties of particulars, existence is at once a property of particulars and a property of properties as well. Existence as a property of particulars (existence$_1$) belongs to a particular by virtue of what a particular is, for all particulars exist$_1$. Existence (existence$_2$), however, does not belong in this way to a property of particulars. Rather existence$_2$ belongs to such a property solely in virtue of a relation which that property bears to something other than itself; for a property of particulars to exist$_2$, some particular must exemplify it. Thus, a property of particulars exists$_2$ when a particular exemplifies it, a property of properties of particulars $exists_3$ when a property of particulars exemplifies it, a property of properties of properties of particulars $exists_4$ when a property of properties of particulars exemplifies it, and so on.

As a result of what might thus be termed the multi-leveled nature of existence, existence statements often pose problems of interpretation of a rather special sort. The negative singular existential (1) is a case in point.

1) Pegasus does not exist.

I will presume that (1) conveys a general proposition,[53] the denial of some relation between the property signified by "Pegasus" and the property signified by "exist". Now "Pegasus" signifies a property of particulars, the property of being Pegasus. But what kind of property does "exist" signify, and what kind of relation is thus denied? If "exist" signifies $existence_1$, then what (1) denies is the <u>inclusion</u> therein of an <u>uniquely exemplified</u> property of particulars, the property of being Pegasus. (1) thus counts as true, since the property of being Pegasus is not exemplified at all. If "exist" signifies $existence_2$, then (1) denies a separate, although related fact: the <u>exemplification</u> of $existence_2$ by a property of particulars, the property of being Pegasus. (1) thus once again counts as true, since a property $exists_2$ only if some particular exemplifies it. Whether "exist" is taken as "$exist_1$" or "$exist_2$", (1) thus counts as true; the interpretations of (1) are mutually entailing, although distinct.

The distinctness in question is a function of the kind of property "exist" in (1) is taken to designate. We can mark this distinctness by

classifying (1) as a proposition of _level 1_ when "exist" ($exist_1$)
signifies a property of particulars, and as a proposition of _level_ 2
when "exist" ($exist_2$) signifies a property of properties of particulars.
In this chapter, we will primarily be concerned with propositions of
level _1_.

Taking "Pegasus" as a property-denoting term and "not" as a
sentence-forming operator,[54] let us accordingly transcribe (1) as

    30) not (PEGASUS $exists_1$).

Now, (30) will correspond to a fact just in case (31) does not.

    31) PEGASUS $exists_1$

Under what conditions will (31) correspond to a fact, and to what kind
of fact will it correspond?

A subject-predicate proposition corresponds to a fact just in case
its subject--its _real_ subject, the ontological one--exists, and is related to the ontological predicate as the proposition says it is. How
any given subject-predicate proposition falls under the foregoing
principle depends on the nature of its terms. Thus, consider (31),
whose ontological subject (hereafter $subject_o$) is not a particular but
a property of particulars. According to our principle, (31) corresponds
to a fact just in case the property of being Pegasus: (i) exists, and
(ii) is included in $existence_1$. This is not quite right, however, for
the _kind_ of existence involved in (i) is not specified. What kind of
existence is this? Since the $subject_o$ of "exists" in (i) is a property
of particulars, "exists" in (1) must be "$exists_2$".[55] (31) thus corresponds to a fact just in case: (i) the property of being Pegasus
$exists_2$; and, (ii) the property of being Pegasus is included in
$existence_1$.

Although logically distinct, conditions (i) and (ii) are not logically independent. Thus consider condition (ii). For the property of being Pegasus to be included in existence$_1$, anything which exemplifies this property must also exemplify existence$_1$. But the property of being Pegasus is a property of <u>particulars</u>. Therefore, anything which exemplifies it will exemplify existence$_1$, since all particulars exist$_1$. <u>Necessarily</u> therefore, the property of being Pegasus is included in existence$_1$.[56] Accordingly, since

$$\text{nec } q \dashrightarrow \text{nec}(p \leftrightarrow p \cdot q),$$

(i) entails--and is entailed by--(i) <u>and</u> (ii). As a result, (31) corresponds to a fact just in case (i) the property of being Pegasus exists$_2$; and (30) corresponds to a fact just in case (31) does not.

Whether (31) corresponds to a fact thus depends upon whether the property of being Pegasus exists$_2$. What in turn conditions the existence$_2$ of the property of being Pegasus?

For a property of particulars to exist$_2$, some particular must exemplify it. If this property is a property of cardinality <u>1</u>, as is the property of being Pegasus, there must be exactly one such particular. The property of being Pegasus thus exists$_2$ just in case one, and only one, thing exemplifies it. As a result, (31) corresponds to a fact just in case one, and only one, thing exemplifies the property of being Pegasus.

So the existence$_1$ of Pegasus discloses upon analysis a series of interconnected relations. First there is the property of being Pegasus, standing in the exemplification relation to existence$_2$, and the inclusion relation to existence$_1$. But the inclusion relation is a feature

66

of every possible relation to existence$_1$ of any property of particulars. So the inclusion relation need not be explicitly imposed as a condition on the relation to existence$_1$ of the property of being Pegasus. Furthermore, a state of affairs wherein the property of being Pegasus stands in the exemplification relation to existence$_2$, also turns out to be a state of affairs wherein one, and only one, thing exemplifies the property of being Pegasus. Thus, the existence$_1$ of Pegasus, and a unique thing's being Pegasus turn out to be distinct but interconnected aspects of the same fact. It is possible to represent this symbolically as in

32) (PEGASUS exists$_1$) ←→ Vx(Px . Λy(Py ←→ y=x))[57].

It should be clear, however, that the right side of (32) is not a logical reconstruction of the propositional content of the left, as Russell would have us believe.

What then of Russell's existence dilemma?

The existence dilemma, recall, arises in connection with the supposition that "Pegasus" is a logical constituent of (1). From this supposition, there is supposed to follow either of two unacceptable consequences. If "Pegasus" is taken to stand for an object, it is supposed that Pegasus will have to stand for a non-existent particular in order for (1) to count as true. If "Pegasus" is not taken to stand for an object, it is supposed that (1) will have to count as meaningless. It should now be evident, however, that the supposition that "Pegasus" stands for an object does not require the acceptance of a non-existent particular.

Let us thus suppose with Russell that: (i) Any object that "Pegasus" might stand for must be capable of functioning as a term of a relation in an atomic fact. To deduce a non-existent particular from (i), it is necessary to introduce a second assumption: (ii) only a _particular_ can function as a term of a relation in an atomic fact. For, from (i) _and_ (ii), but not from (i) alone, it follows that: (iii) "Pegasus" denotes a particular, and hence a non-existent particular, if it denotes at all. It is thus not the supposition that "Pegasus" stands for an object--nor _a_ _fortiori_ the supposition that "Pegasus" is a logical constituent of (1)--which requires that "Pegasus" denote a non-existent particular, if it denotes. It is rather the--as we have argued, ontologically unmotivated--assumption that only a _particular_ can function as a term of a relation in an atomic fact which requires such a conclusion.

2.52 Identity statements

The identity dilemma arises in connection with the supposition that "Scott" and "the author of _Waverley_" are logical constituents of (2).

2) Scott is the author of _Waverley_.

If these terms are taken to stand for objects, (2) is supposed to have to express a necessary truth, despite the apparently contingent identity of Scott and the author of _Waverley_.[58] The only possible justification for such a conclusion, however, would once again seem to be the assumption that these terms cannot stand for _properties_ of particulars.

Let us thus suppose that "Scott" and "the author of _Waverley_" are logical constituents of (2), but that (2) conveys a dyadic _general_ proposition. These terms will then be taken to stand for properties of particulars, and "IS" as signifying inclusion, as in

68

33) SCOTT IS THE AUTHOR OF <u>WAVERLEY</u>.

Under what conditions will (33) correspond to a fact, and to what kind of fact will it correspond?

Designate by <u>S</u> and <u>AW</u> respectively, the property of being Scott and the property of being the author of <u>Waverley</u>. Then (33) corresponds to a fact just in case: (i) <u>S</u> exists$_2$; (ii) <u>AW</u> exists$_2$; and (iii) <u>S</u> is included in <u>AW</u>. Now <u>S</u> and <u>AW</u> will exist$_2$ just in case exactly one thing exemplifies <u>S</u> and exactly one thing exemplifies <u>AW</u>; and <u>S</u> will be included in <u>AW</u> just in case anything which exemplifies <u>S</u> also exemplifies <u>AW</u>. (33) thus corresponds to a fact just in case: exactly one thing is <u>S</u>; exactly one thing is <u>AW</u>; and, anything is <u>S</u> only if it is <u>AW</u>. Symbolically, we thus have, as a necessary and sufficient condition of Scott's being the author of <u>Waverley</u>:

34) $Vx(Sx . \Lambda y(Sy \longrightarrow y=x)) . Vx(AWx . \Lambda y(AWy \longrightarrow y=x)) .$
$\Lambda z(Sx \longrightarrow AWz)$[59]

It is now clear why Scott and the author of <u>Waverley</u> are contingently identical. Although the property of being Scott <u>is</u> included in the property of being the author of <u>Waverley</u>, it is not <u>necessarily</u> included therein, for being the author of <u>Waverley</u> is not a necessary condition on being Scott.

A further ramification of Russell's exclusion of properties as terms of relations is to be found in the following proof of Russell's that "the author of <u>Waverley</u>" has no meaning in isolation (I insert an (a), (b) and (c) for ease of exposition):

> The central point of the theory of descriptions was that a phrase may contribute to the meaning of a sentence without having any meaning at all in isolation. Of this, in the case of descriptions, there is precise proof: (a) If 'the author

of _Waverley_' meant anything other than 'Scott', 'Scott is the author of _Waverley_' would be false, which it is not. (b) If 'the author of _Waverley_' meant 'Scott', 'Scott is the author of _Waverley_' would be a tautology, which it is not. (c) Therefore, 'the author of _Waverley_' means neither 'Scott' nor anything else--i.e. 'the author of _Waverley_' means nothing, Q.E.D."[60]

To interpret this argument correctly, it is necessary to give "means" the sense it acquires within the context of the reference theory of meaning, where a logically significant word or phrase is taken to _mean_ the entity it stands for. Accordingly, we should interpret the premises (a) and (b) and the conclusion (c) as follows: (a') If "the author of _Waverley_" were to stand for a different entity than "Scott", "Scott is the author of _Waverley_" would be false, which it is not. (b') If "the author of _Waverley_" were to stand for the same entity as "Scott", "Scott is the author of _Waverley_" would be a tautology, which it is not. (c') Therefore, "the author of _Waverley_" stands neither for a different nor for the same entity as "Scott"--i.e. "the author of _Waverley_" stands for nothing.

For Russell, the preceding argument provides additional support for the view that a definite description cannot occur significantly as a logical subject. In fact, however, the argument is unsound. Thus, suppose that "the author of _Waverley_" stands for the property of being the author of _Waverley_, and "Scott" for the property of being Scott. These terms will then stand for different entities. But (2) will remain true, nevertheless. Therefore, premise (a') is false. To salvage the argument, it is necessary to suppose that "the author of _Waverley_" and "Scott" denote particulars if they denote at all. In other words, the argument is incomplete without the supposition that (ii) only a _particular_ can function as a term of a relation in an atomic fact.

Frege's famous thesis concerning sense and reference is the out-
come of an argument which Russell's resembles in many respects. Instead
of deploying his argument against the notion that singular terms are
logical constituents of atomic propositions, Frege deploys it against
the notion that the meaning of a singular term is simply the object for
which it stands. Frege's argument, as related by Alston, is as follows:

> Frege's classic example has to do with the expressions 'the
> morning star' and 'the evening star'. They refer to the
> same extralinguistic entity, the planet Venus, but they do
> not have the same meaning. If they did, one could know that
> the morning star is the same entity as the evening star just
> by understanding the meanings of the terms... But this is not
> the case. It was an astronomical discovery that the morning
> star and the evening star are the same... Since meaning can
> vary without a corresponding variation in referent, having
> a meaning cannot consist in referring to a certain object.[61]

Here once again, the tacit assumption is that "the morning star" and
"the evening star" must denote particulars if they denote at all.
Once this is admitted, it follows that the meaning of a term must be
independent of its reference, since the meaning can vary without a corresponding variation in reference. However, if "the morning star" and
"the evening star" are taken as denoting consubstantiated properties,
the premise of Frege's argument turns out to be false. For these terms
will not then, as Frege supposes, have the same denotation. They will
therefore, as predicted by the reference theory of meaning, vary in
meaning as well.

The Fregean critique of a reference theory of meaning, and
Russell's strictures against a subject-predicate logic, are thus both
consequences of a Russell-Frege theory of denoting. According to this
theory, singular terms--whether definite descriptions such as "the

author of Waverley", or proper names such as "Socrates" or "Pegasus"--
correspond to terms of relations in atomic facts. Terms of relations,
moreover, can only be particulars. Therefore, singular terms must denote particulars if they denote at all. Against the Frege-Russell
theory, I have proposed that properties can also function as terms of
relations in atomic facts; and consequently, that singular terms can
also denote properties. This proposal has already been made the basis
of an account of existence and identity statements which involves a
surfacist approach to logical syntax and a reference theory of meaning,
yet does not encounter the problems which Russell and Frege supposed
such an account would engender. This proposal, as we will now see, is
also the basis of an account of singular necessity statements which
avoids the problems cited in connection with (3).

2.53 Necessity statements

Suppose that "nine" and "the number of planets" are logical constituents of (4), (5) and (3), and that "necessarily" functions in (4)
and (3) as a sentence-forming operator. Suppose also that (5), along
with the operands of "necessarily" in (4) and (3), convey general
propositions,[62] as in:

35) necessarily (NINE is odd)

36) NINE is THE NUMBER OF PLANETS

37) necessarily (THE NUMBER OF PLANETS is odd)

Let us, moreover, understand a proposition

$$\text{necessarily } (\pi)[63]$$

to correspond to a fact, just in case "π" corresponds to a fact, and
the constituents of "π" are necessarily related as "π" asserts them to
be.

Accordingly, (35) will correspond to a fact, just in case "NINE is odd" corresponds to a fact, and the constituents of "NINE is odd" are necessarily related as "NINE is odd" asserts them to be. The correspondence-to-fact conditions for (35) are thus that the property of being nine exists$_2$, is included in the property of being odd, and is necessarily so included. Now, the property of being nine exists$_2$, for exactly one thing has that property: nine. The property of being nine is, moreover, included in the property of being odd. Hence, (35) will correspond to a fact just in case the property of being nine is necessarily included in the property of being odd. A property X will be understood to be necessarily included in a property Y, just in case it is not possible for anything to have X without also having Y. (35) thus corresponds to a fact. For nothing can have the property of being nine without also having the property of being odd. (36) also corresponds to a fact, since exactly one thing has the property of being nine, exactly one thing the property of being the number of planets, and these things are the same.

Despite the factuality of (35) and (36), (37) does not correspond to a fact, for the property of being the number of planets is not necessarily included in the property of being odd. Thus, the number nine is necessarily odd. But nine is only contingently the number of planets; conceivably there might have been eight. But eight is not odd. Therefore, a number could conceivably be the number of planets without also being odd. Accordingly, the property of being the number of planets is not necessarily included in the property of being odd. Why (35) and (36) do not jointly entail (37)--nor (4) and (5), (3)--

73

is thus no longer a mystery. By rejecting the Russell-Frege theory of denoting, and allowing "the number of planets" to symbolize a property of a particular as a term of a relation in a general proposition, it is possible to understand (4), (5) and (3) in such a way that the truth of (4) and (5) is consistent with the falsity of (3).

To sum up so far: I am proposing a theory which treats singular terms as logical constituents of the structures which contain them. My theory has thus far been shown to differ from Russell's in two key respects. First, I treat particular and general propositions as atomic-- i.e. subject-predicate in form. For contrary to Russell, I treat the property, not just the particular, as a term of a relation in an atomic fact. I thus maintain that particular and general facts--and propositions--differ essentially in the kinds of things they connect: particular propositions connect particulars and properties, and general propositions, properties and properties: but not in the form of their connection. Russell's claim that, e.g. "The author of Waverley is mortal" conveys a general rather than a particular proposition thus translates, in my theory, into the claim that "the author of Waverley" denotes a property which functions as a term of a relation. Second, I reject a doctrine which is implicit in Russell's treatment of general propositions, and which has emerged as a leading principle in the efforts of many contemporary philosophers to constitute a theory of sentence meaning. According to this doctrine, which I shall refer to as the truth-condition theory, the meaning of a sentence is the set of necessary and sufficient conditions for its truth (as determined by a truth-definition a la Tarski for the language in question). I suggest

74

instead that the meaning of a sentence, i.e. the proposition it expresses, is not identical with, but __determines__ its truth-ground. According to my theory, the truth-ground of a sentence thus has its source in something other than itself.

The obstacles which Russell and Frege place in the way of a subject-predicate logic of singular terms and a reference theory of meaning, I suggest are engendered instead by the limitations which Russell and Frege place upon the reference of singular terms, and hence ultimately by Russell's reluctance to countenance the property as a term of a relation in an atomic fact. These obstacles are thus ontological rather than logical in origin. For they arise from one account, and are resolved by another, of the distribution of particulars and properties inside the context of the atomic fact.

I have thus far restricted my attention to Russell's thesis that general propositions lack logical subjects. In so doing, I have supposed, with Russell, that (A) singular sentences convey general propositions, but do not also convey particular ones. (A) is not a thesis to be taken lightly, however, for it entails that no attempt to describe a particular can ever attain its mark. Thus, the vehicle of such an attempt can only be a particular proposition. Yet in the light of (A), such a proposition cannot be the sense of a singular sentence. Our singular assertions can thus not be about the things they appear to be about. For what we can denote by singular terms are not particulars.

Singular sentences, as Russell claims, convey general propositions. It does not therefore automatically follow, however, that singular sentences do not also convey particular propositions. Bearing in mind the possibility of propositions that are both particular and general, let us consider the line of reasoning which might lead one to conclude that singular sentences do not express particular propositions.

2.6 Singular sentences and particular propositions

2.6.1 Arguments from "exists"

According to Russell, and contrary to what has hitherto been assumed,[64] existence is not a property of particulars:

> ...the individuals that there are in the world do not exist, or rather it is nonsense to say that they exist and nonsense to say that they do not exist.[65]

Why Russell thinks this I will take up shortly. But first I will take up the consequences of this assumption for Russell's analysis of existence statements, and singular sentences generally.

Suppose that it is nonsense to say of a particular that it does or does not exist. Then a significant statement asserting existence, such as, e.g. "The author of Waverley exists", cannot be about a particular. Otherwise, it would be nonsense. Therefore, "the author of Waverley" cannot denote a particular. But neither, for that matter, can any expression of the form "the so-and-so". For a statement "The so-and-so exists" is always significant, which it would not be if "the-so-and-so" denoted a particular. By parity of reasoning, it is possible to demonstrate that no singular term can denote a particular. For it clearly makes sense to couple any singular term--including what are ordinarily counted as proper names--with an assertion or denial of existence. So such expressions cannot denote particulars. But if singular terms do not denote particulars, then neither do singular sentences convey particular propositions.

76

The preceding argument is conclusive only if existence is <u>not</u> a property of particulars. What are Russell's reasons for thinking it is not?

The first reason involves Russell's conception of the difference between a connotative singular term and a genuine proper name--and perhaps his feeling that ordinary proper names ought at times to be capable of behaving like genuine proper names. Thus, a connotative singular term[66] applies to an object as the unique possessor of an attribute or attributes, which the connotative singular term itself signifies. When there is no such object, according to Russell, a connotative singular term continues to occur meaningfully as a predicative component of a propositional function. The meaningfulness of a connotative singular term is thus not tied to its having a denotation.

In contrast, Russell conceives of a genuine proper name as denoting an object without connoting any of its attributes. The meaning of a genuine proper name, unlike that of a connotative singular term, thus consists wholly in its denotation. Therefore, when a genuine proper name lacks a denotation, it cannot occur meaningfully. As plausible a supposition as this might seem, we will now see that it leads directly to the conclusion that if existence <u>is</u> a property of particulars, none of the names we commonly use can be genuine proper names.

Thus, suppose that "b" is a genuine proper name, and has a denotation. Accordingly, "b" will denote a particular, and hence be able to occur meaningfully as the logical subject of a particular proposition. Suppose also that existence is a property of particulars. Then existence will be an __essential__ property, lest some particular, e.g. Pegasus, should fail to exist. As a result, "b exists" is bound to be true, if meaningful. But "b exists" is meaningful, since "b" can occur significantly as the logical subject of a particular proposition, and since existence is a property of particulars. Hence "b exists" is bound to be true. Surely then, "b" cannot be an __ordinary__ proper name. As Ayer points out:

> ...it clearly makes sense...to couple an ordinary proper name with a denial of existence. We can legitimately claim to know that Sir Walter Scott did exist, but anyone who asserted that Scott did not exist would be making a historical, not a logical mistake; his statement would be false, but not nonsensical.[67]

Clearly then, if existence is a property of particulars, none of the names we commonly use can be genuine proper names.

A perhaps more important motive for withholding existence$_1$ from particulars may have been Russell's inability to explain how particulars, which cannot be particulars unless they exist$_1$, nevertheless exist$_1$ __contingently__. In granting existence$_1$ to particulars, what kind of property could Russell have taken it to be? If an __external__ property, a particular might lack existence$_1$ yet still be a particular. But Russell had already taken a firm stand against Pegasus. Yet if Russell construed existence$_1$ as an __internal__ property of particulars, a more serious problem than Pegasus lay in wait: a universe filled with logically necessary existents$_1$. For if existence$_1$ is internal to a particular, then existence$_1$ is a condition on a particular's being what it is:

$$38) \quad \Lambda x \, Nec(x=x \; \dashrightarrow \; EX_1(x))$$

But according to Russell, it is necessarily the case that __everything__ is self-identical:

39) $\mathrm{Nec}\Lambda x(x=x)$

From (38) and (39) it follows that

40) $\Lambda x\ \mathrm{Nec}\ \mathrm{EX}_1(x)$.

Russell avoids the Scylla of non-existent$_1$ particulars and the Charybdis of necessary existents$_1$ by: (i) denying the existence$_2$ of existence$_1$; (ii) making existence$_2$ do the work of existence$_1$;[68] and, (iii) reconstructing existence$_2$ propositions as propositional functions. The details of Russell's reconstructions need not concern us here. What is important to note is that, as in the matter of general proposi- tions, Russell's modus operandi is to eliminate something he does not understand, and cannot explain--namely, existence$_1$; existents$_1$, and the relation which relates them--in favor of something he does.

Existence$_1$ and existents$_1$ aside, the argument against existence statements as particular propositions rests on a key semantical assump- tion: that to occur significantly, a genuine proper name must have a denotation. But, suppose that a name[69] without a denotation can occur significantly. Then the meaningfulness of an existence proposition such as "b exists" will not guarantee its truth. For "b" may not denote.

I will thus propose, contra Russell, that the meaningfulness of a proper name does not depend on its having a denotation. There is now no semantical obstacle to transcribing "Pegasus does not exist" as a particular proposition

41) not (pegasus exists).

(Lower-case spelling indicates the transcription of "Pegasus" as a particular-denoting term.) Now (41) will correspond to a fact just in case (42) does not.

42) pegasus exists

Under what conditions will (42) correspond to a fact, and to what kind
of fact might it correspond?

A monadic particular proposition will correspond to a fact, just
in case: (i) the $subject_o$ $exists_1$; and, (ii) the $subject_o$ exemplifies
the predicate. Note the similarity between the correspondence-to-fact
conditions for particular and general propositions (cf. p. 65). Each
of the conditions (i) requires that the $subject_o$ of a proposition exist;
and each of the conditions (ii) requires that the $subject_o$ be linked
to the predicate by the appropriate ontological tie: exemplification
for the $subject_o$ of a particular proposition and inclusion for the
$subject_o$ of a general proposition.[70] The differences between the consequences of these conditions also reflect the differences between particulars and properties as ontological subjects. Thus, because a
particular is the $subject_o$ of a particular proposition, "exists" in
condition (i) must be $exists_1$, and not $exists_2$ as in condition (i) for
a general proposition. Moreover, since a particular must $exist_1$ in
order to exemplify a property, condition (i) for a particular proposition constitutes a special case of condition (ii). Condition (i) for
a general proposition does not constitute a special case of condition
(ii), however, since the inclusion of property A in property B does not
require that A have instances. (Thus A will be included in B as long
as nothing which has A fails to have B. So if nothing has A, A will
automatically be included in B, since it will not be the case that
something has A and does not have B. In such a case however, A will
not $exist_2$, since it will not have instances.) For the particular

80

proposition (42), we thus have a single correspondence-to-fact condition: (42-ii) pegasus exemplifies existence$_1$.

In general, there are two ways for a particular proposition not to correspond to a fact. Either it can have an ontological subject which does not exemplify the ontological predicate, or it can lack an ontological subject. There is only one way, however, for a particular existence proposition not to correspond to a fact; and that is to lack an ontological subject. For if it has one, the ontological subject of a particular proposition will be a particular, and all particulars exist$_1$. The non-existence of Pegasus is thus reflected by the fact that (42) lacks an ontological subject.

How then shall we reconcile the fact that existence$_1$ is an internal property of particulars with the fact that it is not possible for particulars to exist$_1$ other than contingently? The first fact we can represent as in

43) Nec Λx(x=x $\dashrightarrow$ EX$_1$(x)),

where "x" ranges over particulars; and the second as in

44) $\sim$Pos Vx(Nec(EX$_1$(x))).

(43) and (44) each state an unrevisable truth about particulars. Yet together (43) and (44) entail either that it is not necessary that particulars are self-identical.

45) $\sim$Nec Λx(x=x)

or that it is not possible for there to exist$_1$ particulars

46) $\sim$Pos Vx(EX$_1$(x)).

To see that this is so, we will first establish that (43) and (44), together with the negation of (46), jointly entail (45). Then we will

establish that (43) and (44) together with the negation of (45),
jointly entail (46).

47) ~~To-show~~: [Nec Λx(x=x $\dashrightarrow$ EX_1(x)) . ~Pos Vx(Nec(EX_1(x))) .
Pos Vx(EX_1(x))] $\dashrightarrow$ ~Nec(Λx(x=x))

1.	Nec Λx(x=x $\dashrightarrow$ EX_1(x)) . ~Pos Vx(Nec(EX_1(x))) . Pos Vx(EX_1(x))	Assume
2.	~~Show~~ ~Nec(Λx(x=x))	
3.	Nec Λx(x=x)	Assume
4.	Nec(Λx(x=x) $\dashrightarrow$ Λx(EX_1(x)))	1
5.	Nec Λx(EX_1(x))	3, 4
6.	Nec p $\longleftrightarrow$ (p . Nec p)	
7.	~Pos Vx(EX_1(x) . Nec(EX_1(x)))	1, 6
8.	Pos Vx(EX_1(x) . Nec(EX_1(x)))	1, 5^{71}
9.	~Nec Λx(x=x)	3, 7, 8

48) ~~To-show~~: [Nec Λx(x=x $\dashrightarrow$ EX_1(x)) . ~Pos Vx(Nec(EX_1(x))) .
Nec ΛX(x=x)] $\dashrightarrow$ ~Pos Vx(EX_1(x))

1.	Nec Λx(x=x $\dashrightarrow$ EX_1(x) . ~Pos Vx(Nec(EX_1(x))) . Nec Λx(x=x)	Assume
2.	~~Show~~ ~Pos Vx(EX_1(x))	
3.	Pos Vx(EX_1(x))	Assume
4.	Nec Λx(EX_1(x))	1
5.	Pos Vx(EX_1(x) . Nec(EX_1(x)))	3, 4
6.	Pos Vx(Nec(EX_1(x)))	5
7.	~Pos Vx(EX_1(x))	3, 1, 6

82

As a consequence of the fact that existence$_1$ is an internal property of particulars, and that particulars are contingent existents$_1$, we must thus choose between the necessity that nothing exists$_1$, and the possibility that there is something which is not necessarily self-identical. Life would seem to compel the latter choice. In section 2.9, we will see that this choice is not as dismal as to many philosophers it might seem.

2.62 The argument from the law of the excluded middle

We have seen that arguments from "exists" rest on the supposition that a particular proposition without an ontological subject is unintelligible. The argument from the law of the excluded middle rests on the same supposition. This argument is presented by Russell for the first time in OD. A major criticism of this argument, and an alternative to Russell's analysis of singular terms as incomplete symbols, comes from Strawson in his landmark paper "On Referring" (1950). Russell and Strawson both draw our attention to the semantical ramifications of the non-existence of a present King of France.

Russell's argument runs as follows. Suppose that a grammatically typical connotative singular term such as, e.g. "the present King of France", can function as a logical constituent of a particular proposition "The present King of France is bald". Then, by the law of the excluded middle,

> ...either 'A is B' or 'A is not B' must be true. Hence
> either 'the present King of France is bald' or 'the present
> King of France is not bald' must be true. Yet if we
> enumerated the things that are bald, and then the things
> that are not bald, we should not find the present King of
> France in either list.[72]

Therefore, it would seem that we must either abandon the law of the excluded middle, or conclude that "the present King of France" does not denote a particular. If we conclude that "the present King of France" does not denote a particular, however, we must also conclude that "the present King of France", and hence connotative singular terms generally, cannot function as logical constituents of particular propositions.

The key semantical assumption in the preceding argument is the same assumption which led Russell to conclude that a particular existence proposition "b exists" is bound to be true, if meaningful: that to occur significantly in a particular proposition, a singular term must have a denotation. For otherwise, the presumption that "the present King of France" does not denote a particular fails to license the conclusion that this term cannot occur significantly in the particular proposition "The present King of France is bald".

Strawson objects to the preceding argument on the ground that it incorrectly equates the meaning of a singular term with its reference, and the meaningfulness of a sentence with its viability on a specific occasion of its use. Thus, according to Strawson:

> Meaning...is a function of the sentence or expression; mentioning and referring and truth or falsity are functions of the use of the sentence or expression.[73]

As a result:

> ...the question of whether a sentence or expression is significant or not has nothing whatever to do with the question of whether the expression, uttered on a specific occasion, is...being used to refer to, or mention, anything at all.[74]

Thus, when a logical subject, on a specific occasion of its use, fails to refer, the sentence itself is not spurious, but only the specific use to which it has been put:

> If, when [a person] utters [a sentence], he is not talking
> about anything, then his use is not a genuine one, but a
> spurious or pseudo-use.[75]

By rejecting the notion that the meaning of a sentence can be equated
with the assertion it is used, on a particular occasion, to make,
Strawson is able to reject Russell's contention that the intelligibility
of, e.g. "The present King of France is bald" is tied to "the present
King of France" (_qua_ logical subject)'s having a referent on a specific
occasion of its use. Hence Strawson refuses to see, in the non-
existence of _a so-and-so_, an indication that "the so-and-so" must fail
to exemplify the 'uniquely referring use' characteristic of proper
names and logical subjects.

Strawson thus rejects Russell's argument concerning the inability
of a singular term to function as a logical constituent of a particular
proposition. The fact that Strawson rejects Russell's argument is,
however, not as significant as the extent to which, in so doing, he
concedes the more important of Russell's principles. Thus, for Russell,
the failure of a logical subject to refer results in a sentence's being
unintelligible. For Strawson, on the other hand, failure of a logical
subject (to be used) to refer results in a spurious _use_ of a sentence.
But for Strawson, the intelligibility (meaningfulness) of a sentence
depends on the possibility of its logical subject _having_ a denotation
on a specific occasion of the sentence's use. Hence, a sentence with
a logical subject which cannot be used to refer is just as unintelligible for Strawson as it is for Russell:

> ...the fact that [a sentence] is significant is the same as
> the fact that it _can_ correctly be used to talk about
> something...[76]

85

Thus, for Strawson as for Russell, a subject that <u>can</u> be used to refer is a <u>sine qua non</u> of a meaningful sentence (or proposition):

> The question whether the sentence is significant or not is the question whether there exist such language habits, conventions or rules that the sentence logically could be used to talk about something...[77]

Furthermore, for Strawson as for Russell, that subject must be capable of being used to refer to a <u>particular</u>:

> For a singular referring expression to have a meaning, it suffices that it should be possible in suitable circumstances to use it to refer to some one <u>thing</u>, <u>person</u>, <u>place</u>, &c.[78] [emphasis added]

Thus, for Strawson, sentences like these below with descriptions logically incapable of being used to refer to particulars, should turn out to lack significance.

49) The result of dividing zero by zero is one.

50) An upward falling book is a physical impossibility.

For Russell, on the other hand, the significance of such sentences is not open to question. Although he and Strawson would agree that the possibility of a referring subject is a necessary condition on the significance of subject-predicate sentences, Russell denies such sentences as (49-50) subject-predicate form.

The main disagreement between Strawson and Russell concerns whether a possibly referring subject is, as Strawson proposes, a sufficient as well as necessary condition for a significant subject-predicate sentence, or whether, as Russell's doctrine of singular terms implies, it is only a necessary condition. But this disagreement makes little difference where the assertoric function of a subject-predicate sentence is concerned, since the actual use of such a sentence to make a specific statement or assertion, or to assert a subject-predicate proposition, requires successful singular reference on the part of its logical subject. For Strawson, the actual use of "The present King of France is bald" to make an assertion thus requires that "the present King of France" be used to refer to a particular. Without such a uniquely referring use, this sentence, although meaningful, cannot be used to say anything. Despite Strawson's allowance for the meaningfulness of such a sentence, it is not the possible but the actual existence of a denotation for its logical subject which makes it possible for the sentence to be used to make an assertion. For Strawson as for Russell, it is thus only the actual existence of a denotation for "the present King of France" which makes it possible to say anything about the present King of France.

On the analysis I am proposing, however, the assertoric function of a subject-predicate sentence, qua vehicle of a particular proposition, is subject to no such limitation.[79] Contra Strawson, the particular propositions

51) the present king of france is bald

52) not (the present king of france is bald)

will thus constitute the particular content of sentences which convey something true or false in any epoch, on any occasion of their use. And contra Russell, these sentences will count (in 1981) as false and true, respectively, without requiring there to exist a present King of France.

Now, "the present king of france" is a particular-denoting singular term, which denotes a unique particular, if it denotes. How can we determine whether it denotes? On my analysis, every English singular term is transcribed by both a property-denoting and a particular-denoting singular term. Two such terms which transcribe the same English term correspond. The denotation of the particular-denoting term "the present king of france", if it has one, is then determined by the denotation of the corresponding property-denoting term "THE PRESENT KING OF FRANCE". If some particular exemplifies the property of being the present King of France, "the present king of france" will denote that particular. If there is no such particular, "the present king of france" will not denote.

For (51) to correspond to a fact, its ontological subject must exemplify the property of being bald. For this to be possible, (51) must have an ontological subject. If it does have one, the ontological subject of (51) will be the particular denoted by "the present king of france". But there is no such particular, for no particular exemplifies the property denoted by "THE PRESENT KING OF FRANCE". So (51) does not correspond to a fact. But (51) is the particular proposition conveyed by "The present King of France is bald". So this sentence is false. Since (51) does not correspond to a fact, (52) does. But (52) is the particular proposition conveyed by "The present King of France is not bald", when not is taken as expressing external negation. With negation taken externally, this sentence thus counts as true.

Suppose, however, that negation is taken internally, as in

53) the present king of france is-not bald.

Transcribed as (53) rather than (52), "The present King of France is not bald" conveys a particular proposition whose predicate is excluded

88

from its subject, rather than the negation of a particular proposition whose predicate is attributed to its subject. For (53) to correspond to a fact, its ontological subject must thus exclude (not-exemplify) the property of being bald. But for this to be possible, (53) must have an ontological subject. But (53) does not. So (53) does not correspond to a fact. With negation taken internally, "The present King of France is not bald" counts as false.

2.7 Particular propositions and general propositions

On my analysis, English singular terms have divided reference: an English singular term such as "the author of Waverley" will thus correspond to both the particular-denoting singular term "the author of waverley" and the property-denoting singular term "THE AUTHOR OF WAVERLEY". The copula "is" also signifies a relation whose nature is partially determined by the nature of its terms. When "is" links a particular-denoting term and a predicate, it thus stands for the exemplification relation, and when it links a property-denoting term and a predicate, it stands for the inclusion relation. I will distinguish the "is" of exemplification from the "is" of inclusion by representing the former as "is" and the latter as "IS". I will also transcribe predicate adjectives using upper case spellings, to indicate that predicate adjectives signify properties. Upon analysis, the singular sentence "The author of Waverley is mortal" thus turns out to convey two propositions, one particular and the other general:

54)   the author of waverley is MORTAL

55)   THE AUTHOR OF WAVERLEY IS MORTAL

What is the relation between (54) and (55)?

The particular proposition (54) corresponds to a particular fact, just in case its ontological subject: (i) exists$_1$, and (ii) exemplifies its ontological predicate. The general proposition (55) corresponds to a general fact, just in case its ontological subject: (i) exists$_2$, and (ii) is included in its ontological predicate. Designate by "$\underline{AW}$" and "$\underline{M}$" the properties signified by "THE AUTHOR OF $\underline{WAVERLEY}$" and "MORTAL". Then (54) corresponds to a particular fact, just in case its ontological subject: (i) exists$_1$, and (ii) exemplifies $\underline{M}$. (55) corresponds to a general fact, just in case $\underline{AW}$: (i) exists$_2$, and (ii) is included in $\underline{M}$.

Suppose that (54) corresponds to a particular fact. Then its ontological subject, a particular $\underline{x}$: (i) exists$_1$, and (ii) exemplifies $\underline{M}$. Only $\underline{x}$ has $\underline{AW}$, moreover. Otherwise, "the author of $\underline{waverley}$" would not denote $\underline{x}$,[80] and $\underline{x}$ would not be the ontological subject of (54). Since only one thing has $\underline{AW}$, (i) $\underline{AW}$ exists$_2$. Furthermore, since $\underline{x}$ has $\underline{M}$, and only $\underline{x}$ has $\underline{AW}$, anything which has $\underline{AW}$ also has $\underline{M}$. Hence, (ii) $\underline{AW}$ is included in $\underline{M}$. Thus, (55) corresponds to a general fact, if (54) corresponds to a particular fact.

Now suppose that (55) corresponds to a general fact. Then $\underline{AW}$ (i) exists$_2$, and (ii) is included in $\underline{M}$. So exactly one thing has $\underline{AW}$, a particular $\underline{x}$. Accordingly, "the author of waverley" denotes $\underline{x}$, which (i) exists$_1$. Since $\underline{AW}$ is included in $\underline{M}$, moreover, anything which has $\underline{AW}$ also has $\underline{M}$. Therefore, $\underline{x}$ (ii) exemplifies $\underline{M}$. So the ontological subject of (54): (i) exists$_1$, and (ii) exemplifies $\underline{M}$. So (54) corresponds to a particular fact, just in case (55) corresponds to a general fact. And so it is for such particular and general propositions, generally.

The question why propositions such as (54) and (55) are related in this way requires clarification of the ontological relation between the facts to which they correspond. But clarification of the relation between these facts in turn requires clarification of the relation between their constituents: exemplification and inclusion, and in the case of (54) and (55), the author of waverley and THE AUTHOR OF WAVERLEY. I will not at this point develop these matters as they deserve. I will, however, indicate the nature of the relation which links the entities in question. The relation is one which connects different aspects of the same thing. We will thus see that the author of waverley and THE AUTHOR OF WAVERLEY are different sides of the same particular, exemplification and inclusion different sides of the same relation, the fact that the author of waverley is MORTAL and the fact that THE AUTHOR OF WAVERLEY IS MORTAL different sides of the same fact, (48) and (49) different sides of the same proposition, and "the author of waverley" and "THE AUTHOR OF WAVERLEY" different sides of the same singular term. The relation which makes this so is the identity relation.

Analysis of the identity-relation requires analysis of its terms. I will defer such an analysis to 2.9. At this point, I will set down some facts this analysis will have to explain.

I have suggested that a non-modal singular sentence such as "The author of Waverley is mortal" conveys two propositions, one particular and the other general, as in (54) and (55). I have also suggested that such pairs of propositions correspond, in the sense that (i) their logical subjects each translate the same singular term; and that

(ii) both correspond, or fail to correspond, to a fact. Corresponding pairs of non-modal propositions are thus mutually necessitating. As we will see now, however, corresponding pairs of modal particular and general propositions often correspond or fail to correspond to facts, independently of one another. Let us transcribe "Necessarily, nine is odd" as:

    56) necessarily (nine is ODD)

    57) necessarily (NINE IS ODD)

and, "Necessarily, the number of planets is odd" as:

    58) necessarily (the number of planets is ODD)

    59) necessarily (THE NUMBER OF PLANETS IS ODD)

We will now see that (56, 57) are mutually necessitating, but that (58, 59) are not.

I will understand a particular necessity proposition "necessarily (π)" to correspond to a fact, just in case "π" corresponds to a fact, and its subject$_o$ necessarily exemplifies its predicate$_o$; and a general necessity proposition "necessarily (ϕ)" to correspond to a fact, just in case "ϕ" corresponds to a fact, and its subject$_o$ is necessarily included in its predicate$_o$. I will understand a particular $\underline{x}$ to necessarily exemplify a property $\underline{Y}$, just in case nothing could be $\underline{x}$ without exemplifying $\underline{Y}$. I will understand a property $\underline{X}$ to be necessarily included in a property $\underline{Y}$, just in case nothing could exemplify $\underline{X}$ without exemplifying $\underline{Y}$.[81]

Suppose (57) corresponds to a fact. Denote by "$\underline{N}$" and "$\underline{O}$" the properties signified by "NINE" and "ODD". Then, (i) $\underline{N}$ exists$_2$ and is included in $\underline{O}$; and, (ii) $\underline{N}$ is necessarily included in $\underline{O}$. Hence, for exactly one number x, x exemplifies N. Call that number "a". Now N is necessarily included in O. It does not therefore follow, however, that a exemplifies O necessarily. To show that a exemplifies O necessarily, we must show that

60) necessarily (a is NINE)

corresponds to a fact: that nothing could be a if it did not exemplify N.

To dispel suspicion of a confusion, consider the case of Mary's husband. Call him "b". Would it be possible for b, Mary's husband, not to be Mary's husband? Now this question does not concern the assertibility of a propositional function. Nor does it concern whether "Mary's husband" is a rigid designator.[82] It concerns b, the person who is Mary's husband, and so, the factuality of the particular proposition conveyed by "Necessarily, Mary's husband is Mary's husband":

61) necessarily (mary's husband is MARY'S HUSBAND)

For the factuality of (61) turns on nothing other than whether b, who is Mary's husband, has the property of being Mary's husband necessarily or contingently. Similarly, the factuality of (60) turns on nothing other than whether a has the property of being nine necessarily or contingently.

Accordingly, (60) will correspond to a fact, just in case: (i) a exemplifies N; and, (ii) a necessarily exemplifies N. We already have that a is the unique number x which exemplifies N. So a exemplifies N. But does a exemplify N necessarily? If not, then it would be possible for a to be a without exemplifying N. In other words, it would be possible for the number which exemplifies the property of being nine, not to exemplify that property. But this is not possible. Accordingly, (60) corresponds to a fact.

Returning to (56, 57): we have, by hypothesis, that (i) $\underline{N}$ exists$_2$ and is included in $\underline{O}$; and that (ii) $\underline{N}$ is necessarily included in $\underline{O}$. Hence, exactly one number, namely $\underline{a}$, exemplifies $\underline{N}$. By (60), moreover, $\underline{a}$ exemplifies $\underline{N}$ necessarily. So it is not possible for anything to be $\underline{a}$ without having $\underline{N}$. Therefore, by (ii), $\underline{a}$ exemplifies $\underline{O}$ necessarily. But $\underline{a}$ is the subject of "nine is ODD" in (56). Hence, (56) corresponds to a fact, if (57) does.

Suppose (56) corresponds to a fact. Then for exactly one number $\underline{x}$: (i) $\underline{x}$ has $\underline{N}$; and (ii) $\underline{x}$ has $\underline{O}$ necessarily. Call this number "$\underline{a}$". Now for $\underline{N}$ to be necessarily included in $\underline{O}$, it must be the case that nothing could have $\underline{N}$ without having $\underline{O}$. But $\underline{N}$ is an _essence_ of $\underline{a}$, in Plantinga's sense.[83] Thus, $\underline{a}$ not only has $\underline{N}$ essentially. $\underline{N}$ is also necessarily _unique to_ $\underline{a}$. That is, nothing could have $\underline{N}$ without _being_ $\underline{a}$. Therefore, since $\underline{a}$ has $\underline{O}$ necessarily, and $\underline{N}$ is necessarily unique to $\underline{a}$, $\underline{N}$ is necessarily included in $\underline{O}$. That is, no number could have $\underline{N}$ without also having $\underline{O}$. Therefore, (57) corresponds to a fact, if (56) does.

So (56) and (57) are mutually necessitating. But they are not mutually necessitating as a matter of logical necessity innocent of ontological content. Quite to the contrary, their mutual necessitation takes its rise from an ontological _fact_: that nine is what it is essentially, and not otherwise.

Now, nine _is_ the number of planets. But unlike nine, which is essentially _nine_, the number of planets is not essentially the number

of planets. As a result, the particular proposition (58) can correspond to a fact, while the general proposition (59) does not.

Consider the particular propositions:

62) necessarily (the number of planets is THE NUMBER OF PLANETS)

63) the number of planets is THE NUMBER OF PLANETS

The proposition (62) asserts that the number of planets is what it is
essentially. The factuality of (62) thus rests upon the necessary
factuality of (63). The logical subject $\underline{and}$ predicate of (63) are of
specified cardinality. Taking cardinality into account, we have for
(63) the correspondence-to-fact conditions: (i) the subject$_o$ exists$_1$;
(ii) the predicate$_o$ exists$_2$; and (iii) the former exemplifies the
latter. Of these, moreover, any one can do the work of the other two.[84]
In the place of (i) and (ii), we will thus take: (iii) the number of
planets exemplifies the property of being the number of planets. The
factuality of (62) will then turn upon whether this property is
exemplified necessarily.

We will denote by "$\underline{NP}$" the property of being the number of
planets, and by "$\underline{a}$" either the unique number which exemplifies this
property, or if there is no such number, nothing. So (62) will cor-
respond to a fact, just in case: (i) $\underline{a}$ exemplifies $\underline{NP}$; and, (ii)
$\underline{a}$ exemplifies $\underline{NP}$ necessarily. Assume that for exactly one number $\underline{x}$,
$\underline{x}$ exemplifies $\underline{NP}$. Then $\underline{x}$ is $\underline{a}$. So (i) $\underline{a}$ exemplifies $\underline{NP}$. Hence (63)
corresponds to a fact. For that fact to be a $\underline{necessary}$ one, however,
it must be the case that no number $\underline{could}$ be $\underline{a}$ unless that number exemplified $\underline{NP}$. But this means that $\underline{a}$ could not be $\underline{a}$ unless $\underline{a}$ exemplified $\underline{NP}$. But this is absurd. So the fact which corresponds to (63)

is a _contingent_ fact. Therefore, the fact that the number of planets is necessarily the number of planets is not a fact at all. As we will now see, the contingent identity of the number of planets finds its expression in the ontological independence of (58, 59).

Suppose that (59) corresponds to a fact. Then, (i) NP exists$_2$ and is included in O; and, (ii) NP is necessarily included in O. Hence, for exactly one number x, x has NP. Call this number "a". So a has NP, and NP is necessarily included in O. It does not therefore follow, however, that a has O necessarily. For a to have O necessarily, it would have to be so that a could not possibly _not_ have NP. But no number is _necessarily_ the number of planets. As a result of the contingent identity of the number of planets, (59) fails to necessitate (58).[85]

Now suppose that (58) corresponds to a fact. Then, np has O necessarily. Hence, for exactly one number x, x has NP. Call this number "a". Since only a has NP, NP exists$_2$. Since a has NP and O, NP is included in O. Since np has O necessarily, and a is np, a has O necessarily. It does not therefore follow, however, that NP is necessarily included in O. For this to be the case, anything that _could_ have NP would have to have O. But, just because a has NP does not mean no other number _could_ have NP: NP is not _necessarily_ unique to a. Once again, therefore, as a result of the _contingent_ identity of the number of planets, the factuality of (58) is consistent with the non-factuality of (59).

But how is contingent identity possible? Is not identity, as Dummett puts it, "the minimal reflexive relation between objects"[86] and so a relation which every object bears, necessarily, only to itself, and bears to itself necessarily? And given the necessary character of self-identity:

(i) Nec $\wedge x(x=x)$

are not identical things necessarily identical? For, given Leibniz's principle of the indiscernibility of identicals

(ii) $\wedge x \wedge y((x=y) \dashrightarrow (F(x) \leftrightarrow F(y)))$,[87]

we get, by substituting for the letter "F" the property being identical with x:

(iii) $\wedge x \wedge y((x=y) \dashrightarrow [Nec(x=x) \leftrightarrow Nec(y=x)])$

Now it follows from (i) that

(iv) $\wedge x\ Nec(x=x)$.

But from (iii) and (iv), it follows that

(v) $\wedge x \wedge y[(x=y) \dashrightarrow Nec(y=x)]$.

The property being identical with x thus entails the modal property being necessarily identical with x. Identity with any particular object must therefore be an internal relation.

The concluding section of this chapter will be devoted to an analysis of identity which invalidates the preceding argument. I will show that identity is a relation which holds between different aspects of the same thing. I will thus argue that because certain aspects of a thing are not essential to it, premise (i) is false. Premise (ii), which posits the indiscernibility of identicals, I will argue is also false. For indiscernibility rests on sameness, while within identicals there is also difference. The conclusion that identity is an internal relation, I will thus show to be unwarranted on two grounds: that self-identity can be contingent, and that identity involves difference.

To get clear what kind of relation the identity-relation is, let us first shed some light on the nature of its terms.

2.8 The particular

My analysis of the identity-relation posits a particular which, unlike Russell's, is two-sided and multi-faceted. Russell's particular, it will be recalled,[88] is logically simple and essentially bare. Since its nature is not to have a nature, it has no essential properties or relations. The logically proper symbol for Russell's particular is thus one which names but does not describe.

My particular, in contrast, encloses within itself an intrinsic qualitative definiteness. Since it has a nature, it is logically complex, and has essential properties and relations. The logically proper symbol for my particular must thus both name and describe.

The constituents of such a particular are present in Russell's PM theory of denoting, but the particular itself is not. In PM, a connotative singular term indicates a concept, which in turn "denotes" an object. The concept is a universal, a fragment of the qualitative definiteness of a particular. The object is an individual, the ground of that qualitative definiteness. But the particular itself is missing. For the particular has been bifurcated into two of its complementary aspects, the individual and the universal--an existence and a content-- each now existing, impossibly, outside of its connection with the particular, and each therefore lacking any internal interrelation with the other.

The ontological presuppositions of Russell's bifurcation of the particular reveal themselves in the successive phases of his elimination of the particular as an ontological subject. In PM, a connotative

singular term still symbolizes, indirectly, both aspects of the bifur-

cated particular, the denoting concept and its object. Yet even at

this stage, the concept cannot function as a term of a proposition. The

qualitative definiteness of the particular has thus already been elimi-

nated as a term of a relation in a general fact. In OD, the tie linking

denoting concept and object is severed, and the qualitative definiteness

of the particular exported to the ontological predicate. All that now

remains of the particular as an ontological subject is the individual,

a bare particular which can neither be named nor described.[89]

The bifurcation of the particular entails a bifurcation of its

relations. First, the identity relation between the particular and

each of its properties is bifurcated into its complementary sides: an

exemplification relation linking an individual--a bare particular--and

an unparticularized universal,[90] and an inclusion relation linking un-

particularized universals. Then, consequent upon the exclusion of the

unparticularized universal from the ontological subject, the inclusion

relation is itself eliminated in favor of classes of exemplification

relations. The Russellian dialectic has run its course.

Restoration of the particular as an ontological subject thus

calls for a reversal of the Russellian dialectic. The first stages of

that reversal have already been accomplished. The qualitative definite-

ness of the particular has been retrieved from among its predicates, and

placed alongside the individual as a term of a relation in an atomic

fact. The inclusion relation has been reconstituted from classes of

exemplification relations, and placed alongside of exemplification as the characteristic mode of connection of the constituents of a general fact. Consequent upon these steps, a property-denoting singular term has been retrieved from the predicative component of the propositional function, and placed alongside of its particular-denoting counterpart as the logical subject of a general proposition.

But the reversal of the Russellian dialectic requires completion. Although the individual and the universal once again exist side-by-side as terms of relations in atomic facts, they are separate entities, a bare particular and an unparticularized universal, rather than complementary sides of the same qualitatively definite particular. Although exemplification and inclusion once again exist side-by-side as the characteristic modes of connection of the constituents of particular and general facts, they are separate relations rather than complementary sides of the same relation. Although corresponding non-modal particular and general facts and propositions are mutually necessitating, their connection is unexplained, since they are separate facts and propositions rather than complementary sides of the same facts and propositions. Finally, although the denotation of a particular-denoting singular term is determined by the denotation of the corresponding property-denoting singular term, the correspondence of such terms is totally mysterious, since such terms are separate expressions rather than complementary sides of the same expression.

The reversal of the Russellian dialectic thus requires for its completion the reconstitution of the individual and the universal as complementary aspects of a self-same particular. Once the Russellian bifurcation of the particular is finally undone, exemplification and inclusion will be seen as complementary sides of a self-same identity-relation, corresponding particular and general facts and propositions as complementary sides of facts and propositions that are both particular and general, and corresponding particular- and property-denoting singular terms as complementary sides of a singular term capable of embracing both sides of any particular it names.

The complex has been extracted from the simple. Let us now find the simple in the complex.

2.9   The identity-relation

To be a particular is to be qualitatively definite. A given particular stands in the identity-relation to its qualitative definiteness. For this definiteness is the definiteness of that particular. Thus, consider the author of Waverley, whose qualitative definiteness qua the author of Waverley consists in the fact that he is the author of Waverley. We thus have the formal identity statement:[91]

64) The author of Waverley is the author of Waverley.

Now, on our analysis, one of the occurrences of "the author of Waverley" may be understood as referring to the author of Waverley, and the other as referring to the property of being the author of Waverley, as in:

65) The author of Waverley is THE AUTHOR OF WAVERLEY

As previously, I use upper-case spelling to indicate that a term signifies a universal.[92] In (65), however, I depart from previous practise in one significant respect: I underscore a term which indicates, not an aspect of a particular, but the particular itself. An example will help to illustrate this point.

Thus, consider Mary's husband. Call him "b". Taking "Mary's

husband" and "b" as logical subjects of the same identity-proposition, we thus have:

66) **Mary's husband** is MARY'S HUSBAND

67) b is MARY'S HUSBAND

Now, the ontological subject of (66) is Mary's husband, a particular. The particular in question is complete with respect to the property of being Mary's husband, because it 'already' encloses within itself that property. In contrast, the ontological subject of (67) is b, that aspect of the particular Mary's husband which stands in the exemplification relation to the property of being Mary's husband. In other words, with respect to the property of being Mary's husband, but--and here I emphasize--only with respect to this property, b is an individual, a bare particular. Therefore, (67) asserts something informative when it asserts that b exemplifies this property, because b is incomplete with respect to the property in question. In contrast, (66) is both informative and redundant. It is informative because in being about the particular Mary's husband, it is also about one of its aspects, the individual b, which is incomplete with respect to the property of being Mary's husband, and which, it asserts, exemplifies this property. It is redundant because in being about this particular, it is also about its complementary aspect, the property--a universal--of being Mary's husband, which it asserts, redundantly, is included in itself.

The individual b is therefore the result of extruding a universal from a particular: the property of being Mary's husband from Mary's husband. Thus, schematically:

68) **Mary's husband** - MARY'S HUSBAND = b

But this is not quite right. For, as noted above, b is an individual, a bare particular, only with respect to the property of being Mary's husband. The other properties which Mary's husband has, the relative particular b also has. Thus, schematically:

69) Mary's husband - MARY'S HUSBAND = mary's husband

70) Mary's husband - mary's husband = MARY'S HUSBAND

The term "mary's husband" thus signifies a relative particular, an entity which is 'bare' with respect to the property of being Mary's husband, but is otherwise a full-fledged particular in its own right.

Before we attempt a full-scale analysis of the identity-relation, it will be useful to introduce the full range of objects, relations and symbols such an analysis requires. Our analysis requires the following objects: particulars, relative particulars, and universals. A particular is an individual thing or event. A universal is a part or aspect of a particular which can in principle also characterize other particulars. A relative particular can be a particular, or relative particular, from which a universal has been extruded. (Alternatively, as we will see below, a particular can be a relative particular which exemplifies no universals, a maximal relative particular as it were). A particular exists simpliciter; universals and relative particulars exist only as aspects of particulars.

To indicate that an object is a particular, we will underline the term which refers to it. To refer to the particular the author of Waverley, we will thus employ the term "the author of Waverley". To indicate that an object is a relative particular, we will eschew underlining and employ lower-case spelling. The result of extruding, from the particular <u>the</u> <u>author</u> <u>of</u> <u>Waverley</u>, the property--a universal--of being <u>the</u> <u>author</u> <u>of</u> <u>Waverley</u>, is thus the relative particular the author of waverley. To refer to this relative particular we will employ the term "the author of waverley". Finally, to indicate that an object is a universal, we will employ upper-case spelling. The result of extruding, from the particular <u>the</u> <u>author</u> <u>of</u> <u>Waverley</u>, the relative particular the author of waverley, is thus the universal THE AUTHOR OF WAVERLEY. To refer to this universal, we will employ the term "THE AUTHOR OF WAVERLEY".

In addition to the foregoing objects and their symbols, our analysis will require a number of relations. The first of these is the identity-relation, which we will symbolize by "<u>is</u>". The identity-relation is, as Dummett puts it, "the minimal reflexive relation between objects", which any particular or relative particular[93] bears only to itself. The second relation we will require holds between any (relative) particular and a universal which it <u>embodies</u>. Thus, in "<u>Mary's</u> <u>husband</u> is MARY'S HUSBAND", the particular <u>Mary's</u> <u>husband</u> embodies the universal MARY'S HUSBAND. The relative particular mary's husband, however, does <u>not</u> embody MARY'S HUSBAND, for mary's husband arises from <u>Mary's</u> <u>husband</u> as a result of the <u>extrusion</u> of MARY'S HUSBAND. The embodiment-relation we will symbolize by "<u>is</u>". Our third relation will hold between a (relative) particular and any <u>relative</u> particular which it <u>contains</u>. Thus, the particular <u>Mary's</u> <u>husband</u> contains the relative particular mary's husband, the latter arising from the former as a result of the extrusion of the universal MARY'S HUSBAND. Conversely, the relative particular mary's husband is contained in Mary's husband. No relative particular contains itself, however; the containment-relation can hold only between a (relative) particular and the result of extruding some universal therefrom. The containment-relation we will symbolize by "$\overline{is}$". Our fourth relation will hold between a relative particular x and universal f, just in case for some (relative) particular x', x arises from x' as a result of the extrusion of f. This relation, which we will symbolize by "is", is the exemplification-relation. Schematically, we thus have

71) is(x, f) $\iff$ Vx'(x' - f = x).

The exemplification-relation thus holds between the relative particular mary's husband and the universal MARY'S HUSBAND, for mary's husband arises from Mary's husband as a result of the extrusion of MARY'S HUSBAND. This relation, however, does not hold between Mary's husband and MARY'S HUSBAND, nor does it hold between any (relative) particular and a property it embodies. The reason for this is straightforward. If a (relative) particular were to exemplify and embody some property f, it could not arise, as required by (71), as a result of the extrusion of f; for if it did, it would not embody f. Our fifth relation holds between universals f, g such that every relative particular which ex-emplifies f also exemplifies g. This is the inclusion relation, which we will symbolize by "IS". Our sixth, and last relation holds between any universal f and relative particular x such that x exemplifies f. This relation, which we will symbolize by "iš", is converse exemplification.

To summarize the preceding in tabular form:

RELATION	RELATA	SYMBOL
IDENTITY	a (relative) particular and itself	$\underline{is}$
EMBODIMENT	a (relative) particular and universal	is
CONTAINMENT	a (relative) particular and relative particular	$\overline{is}$
EXEMPLIFICATION	a relative particular and universal	is
INCLUSION	a universal and a universal	IS
CONVERSE EXEMPLIFICATION	a universal and relative particular	$\overset{\smile}{is}$

72)

Each of these relations, as we will now see, is involved in the self-identity of the author of Waverley, and indeed of any other particular.

The particular the author of Waverley, like any other such, is a unity of two complementary aspects, a what and a that, a universal and a relative particular, THE AUTHOR OF WAVERLEY and the author of waverley. To relate the author of Waverley to itself, as in

73) the author of Waverley $\overline{is}$ the author of Waverley,

is thus to relate the author of Waverley to each of its complementary aspects: THE AUTHOR OF WAVERLEY and the author of waverley. One side of the identity-relation asserted in (73) is thus the relation asserted to hold between the author of Waverley and THE AUTHOR OF WAVERLEY:

74) the author of Waverley is THE AUTHOR OF WAVERLEY

This is the embodiment-relation: a particular is asserted to embody a universal. The other side of the identity-relation is the relation asserted to hold between the author of Waverley and the author of waverley:

75) the author of Waverley $\overline{is}$ the author of waverley

This is the containment-relation: a particular is asserted to contain a relative particular. Upon analysis, the identity-relation thus resolves itself into its two complementary sides: the embodiment-relation and the containment-relation.

The embodiment-relation and the containment-relation are each in turn susceptible of further analysis. Thus, to relate the author of Waverley to THE AUTHOR OF WAVERLEY, as in (74), is also to relate each of this particular's complementary aspects, a relative particular and a universal, to THE AUTHOR OF WAVERLEY. One side of the embodiment-relation is thus the relation asserted to hold between the author of waverley and THE AUTHOR OF WAVERLEY:

76) the author of waverley is THE AUTHOR OF WAVERLEY

This is the exemplification-relation: a relative particular is asserted to exemplify a universal. The other side of the embodiment-relation is the relation asserted to hold between THE AUTHOR OF WAVERLEY and THE AUTHOR OF WAVERLEY:

77) THE AUTHOR OF WAVERLEY IS THE AUTHOR OF WAVERLEY

This is the inclusion-relation: a universal is asserted to be included in a universal. Upon analysis, the embodiment-relation thus likewise resolves itself into its two complementary sides: the exemplification-relation and the inclusion-relation.

The containment-relation also has two complementary sides. To relate the author of Waverley to the author of waverley, as in (75), is also to relate each complementary aspect of this particular to the author of waverley. One side of the containment-relation is thus the relation asserted to hold between THE AUTHOR OF WAVERLEY and the author of waverley:

78) THE AUTHOR OF WAVERLEY is the author of waverley

This relation is <u>converse</u> <u>exemplification</u>: a universal is asserted to be exemplified in a relative particular. The other side of the containment-relation is the relation asserted to hold between the author of waverley and the author of waverley:

79) the author of waverley <u>is</u> the author of waverley

This relation is, once again, the identity-relation: a relative particular is asserted to be identical with itself. The complementary sides of the containment-relation are thus the converse exemplification-relation and the identity-relation.

In the light of the preceding analysis, two hitherto puzzling features of the identity-relation receive their explanation: its <u>possible</u> <u>contingency</u> and its <u>informativeness</u>. As evidenced in (76) and (78), the identity of the author of <u>Waverley</u> <u>does</u> involve a contingent aspect: the fact that the author of waverley and THE AUTHOR OF WAVERLEY are aspects of the <u>same</u> particular. The potential <u>informativeness</u> of "The author of <u>Waverley</u> is the author of <u>Waverley</u>" thus arises from the nature of the relation which this statement asserts. At the heart of the identity of the author of <u>Waverley</u> is the fact that the relative particular the author of waverley, which does not <u>embody</u> the property of <u>being</u> the author of <u>Waverley</u>, nevertheless <u>exemplifies</u> this property. To become aware of the identity of the author of <u>Waverley</u> is thus to become aware of the unity of a relative particular and a property which it does <u>not</u> embody, a unity which arises from the fact that the relative particular and property are aspects of the <u>same</u> particular.

To see that <u>contingent</u> identity is involved in the identity of the author of <u>Waverley</u>, imagine that the author of <u>Waverley</u> had not authored <u>Waverley</u>. In this circumstance, <u>he</u> would have the property of not having authored <u>Waverley</u>. Of whom are we speaking? The author of <u>Waverley</u>. But the author of <u>Waverley</u> we have in mind does not embody the property of <u>being</u> the author of <u>Waverley</u>. <u>That</u> property we have extruded, <u>thus</u>:

80) the <u>author</u> <u>of</u> <u>Waverley</u> - THE AUTHOR OF WAVERLEY =

the author of waverley

Is "The author of <u>Waverley</u> is the author of <u>Waverley</u>" therefore a contingent proposition? It <u>is</u> contingent on the side leading from the individual (the "relative particular") to the universal--from the author of waverley to THE AUTHOR OF WAVERLEY--since these need <u>not</u> have been aspects of the <u>same</u> particular. But, on its other two sides-- leading from THE AUTHOR OF WAVERLEY to THE AUTHOR OF WAVERLEY, and from the author of waverley to the author of waverley--this proposition is necessary. For its terms are not only <u>identical</u>, they are <u>the</u> <u>same</u>. Our proposition is thus both contingent <u>and</u> necessary, depending upon which side it is viewed from. Its <u>contingent</u> side, however, is its <u>informative</u> side, the side which links a relative particular and a universal, thus conveying something about the world of a non-formal nature. Its necessary side, in contrast is uninformative because redundant. It could hardly be otherwise. For the identity of its terms excludes their difference.

From this, however, it does not follow that all necessary identity-propositions are uninformative. To convince ourselves of this, we need only consider the necessary proposition

81) Scott $\overline{is}$ Scott.

Now, (81) relates Scott and Scott. But in so doing, it also relates,
ultimately, Scott's complementary aspects:

82)   scott is SCOTT

83)   SCOTT IS SCOTT

84)   scott $\overline{is}$ scott

(83) and (84), like (77) and (79), are necessary and uninformative, and
so need concern us no further. In (82), however, the relative particular scott is asserted to exemplify a universal, the property of being
Scott. To judge whether the relation between scott and SCOTT is contingent or necessary, and whether the assertion of this relation is
informative or redundant, we need to get clear what is involved in being Scott.

To be Scott is to be a thing, distinct from other things. To be
Scott is thus to have a kind of property that each distinct thing has,
simply by virtue of the fact that it is a distinct thing. But to be
Scott is not to be just any distinct thing. It is to be some distinct
thing, and not another one. To be Scott is thus to exemplify a
specific instance of the property of being a particular. To learn that
Scott is Scott, in the sense conveyed by (82), is thus not to become
acquainted with a tautology. It is to learn which specific instance of
the property of being a particular the relative particular scott exemplifies. In other words, to learn that Scott is Scott is to learn
which specific person Scott is.[94] It does not therefore follow, however, that the connection between scott and SCOTT is a contingent one.

Since "SCOTT" signifies a specific instance of the property of being a particular: (i) it individuates, necessarily, the particular which has it; and, (ii) it is an essential property of that particular. Thus, not only is nobody other than Scott Scott; nobody other than Scott could be Scott. The property of being Scott is thus necessarily unique to Scott. Furthermore, if Scott were not Scott, Scott would not be. The relative particular scott in (82) would thus cease to exist. Therefore, the property of being Scott is an essential property of Scott. Since SCOTT is necessarily unique to Scott, and essential in Scott, SCOTT is, in Plantinga's sense, an essence of Scott. The relation involved in (82) is thus internal to the relative particular scott. Therefore, the proposition "Scott is Scott" is necessary on each of its three sides; i.e., in (82) as well as in (83), and (84). Thus, the identity of Scott, unlike the identity of the author of Waverley, is necessary--even though, as we must not forget, Scott and the author of Waverley are one and the same. Self-identity may thus be necessary or contingent, depending only on the nature of the self-identical thing. Therefore, since the doctrine that identity is an internal relation rests on the premise that necessarily everything is self-identical, the doctrine that identity is an internal relation rests on a mistake.

The basis of that mistake is the notion that identity excludes difference. For the identity of an object consists, essentially, in the relation in which it stands to what it is. Identity, therefore, posits a difference in its terms. The relation of, e.g. the author of Waverley to the author of Waverley thus involves, in addition to the

111

trivial self-relation of THE AUTHOR OF WAVERLEY and THE AUTHOR OF WAVERLEY, and the author of waverley and the author of waverley, the non-trivial, and contingent relation of the relative particular the author of waverley to the universal THE AUTHOR OF WAVERLEY. But these terms are both identical and different. They are identical because they are aspects of the same thing. They are different because they are different aspects of that thing.

Identity that excludes difference can only consist in the self-relation of an unparticularized universal or a bare particular. Such identity must be necessary, for what is there that could change about either of these relations? Identity that includes difference, however, consists in the relation of a relative particular to a universal. Such identity can therefore be either necessary or contingent, depending on the nature of its terms.

We have seen that identity which excludes difference is the only kind of identity that can be appealed to in support of the notion that things are necessarily self-identical. We will now see that this kind of identity is also at the heart of a second shibboleth of modern philosophy, Leibniz's principle of the indiscernibility of identicals. This principle holds that when two things are one and the same, every property of one is also a property of the other.

Thus, consider the case of two such things, Hesperus and Phosphorus, which the ancient Greeks believed to be distinct heavenly bodies. According to Leibniz's principle, such a belief should have been impossible: the identity of Hesperus and Phosphorus should have resulted in their indiscernibility, such that every belief about one was also a belief about the other. Such evidently was not the case,

however, for it is fair to assume that the ancients' belief that

Hesperus and Phosphorus were distinct was not accompanied by the belief

that, e.g. Phosphorus and Phosphorus were distinct. Defenders of the

indiscernibility of identicals have sought to account for the possi-

bility of belief in the distinctness of identicals in one of two ways.

They have either, like Frege, made out the denotation of e.g.,

"Hesperus" and "Phosphorus" in belief contexts to be something other

than the ordinary reference of these terms, or they have denied, like

Russell, that such terms are logical constituents of the propositions

in whose verbal expressions they occur. In either case, the result is

the same: the elimination of Hesperus and Phosphorus as epistemological

objects of belief. The account I have in mind, on the other hand, pre-

serves Hesperus and Phosphorus as epistemological objects of belief,

while rejecting the indiscernibility of identicals.

Thus consider the identity-statement:

85) Hesperus $\overline{\text{is}}$ Phosphorus

Selecting "Hesperus" as the logical subject of (85), we have the

transcriptions;

86) hesperus is PHOSPHORUS

87) HESPERUS IS PHOSPHORUS

88) hesperus $\overline{\text{is}}$ phosphorus

and selecting "Phosphorus" as the logical subject, we have:

89) phosphorus is HESPERUS

90) PHOSPHORUS IS HESPERUS

91) phosphorus $\overline{\text{is}}$ hesperus

With respect to (85-91), I shall try to establish the following results: (i) hesperus and phosphorus are identical; (ii) hesperus and phosphorus are absolutely identical; (iii) HESPERUS and PHOSPHORUS are relatively identical. In the light of (i-iii), I will then try to motivate the following epistemological conclusions: (iv) (86), (89) and (87, 90) are distinct and independent objects of belief; (v) (87) and (90) are distinct but mutually necessitating objects of belief; and, (vi) neither (85), (88) nor (91) unanalyzed, are possible objects of belief.

(i) To show that hesperus and phosphorus are identical, it will suffice to show that they are aspects of the same particular. By property extrusion, we thus have:

92) Hesperus - HESPERUS = hesperus

93) Phosphorus - PHOSPHORUS = phosphorus

Now, hesperus is like Hesperus except in not embodying HESPERUS, and phosphorus like Phosphorus except in not embodying PHOSPHORUS. If we can now show that hesperus also fails to embody PHOSPHORUS, and phosphorus HESPERUS, we will have shown that hesperus and phosphorus are identical. To see that hesperus fails to embody PHOSPHORUS, and phosphorus HESPERUS, we need only consider (86) and (89), according to which hesperus exemplifies PHOSPHORUS, and phosphorus HESPERUS. As has previously been established (cf. p. 105), no relative particular can embody and exemplify the same property. Therefore, hesperus lacks PHOSPHORUS, and phosphorus HESPERUS. Hence, since hesperus and phosphorus arise from identicals by extrusion of the same properties, hesperus and phosphorus are identicals. Schematically:

94) Hesperus - HESPERUS - PHOSPHORUS = hesperus

Phosphorus - PHOSPHORUS - HESPERUS = phosphorus

Hesperus = Phosphorus

hesperus = phosphorus

(ii) The identity of hesperus and phosphorus resides in the fact that they are aspects of the same particular. Their absolute identity will reside in the fact that they are the same aspect of that particular. Now, for hesperus and phosphorus to be different aspects of that particular, hesperus and phosphorus would have to have aspects that were different, just as, e.g. being Hesperus and being Phosphorus constitute different aspects of one and the same particular. But the difference between Hesperus and Phosphorus resides in the difference between the universals HESPERUS and PHOSPHORUS. But, it is precisely these universals, HESPERUS and PHOSPHORUS, which have been extruded from Hesperus and Phosphorus to arrive at the relative particulars hesperus and phosphorus. The identity of hesperus and phosphorus thus excludes difference. The relative particulars hesperus and phosphorus are therefore not only identical, but absolutely identical, for they are the same aspect of the same particular.

(iii) The universals HESPERUS and PHOSPHORUS are identical in that they are aspects of the same particular. They are relatively identical in that they are different aspects of that particular. For the property of being Hesperus and the property of being Phosphorus are two distinct instances of the same universal: the property of being a thing distinct from other things. That one and the same thing should harbor distinct instances of the same property should be no cause for

surprise. For each such instance is a fragment of that particular's
individual nature. To grasp the identity of HESPERUS and PHOSPHORUS,
as in (87), is thus to grasp the fact that the same relative particular
exemplifies the universals in question.

(iv) It follows from (iii) that (86) and (89) are epistemologically distinct and epistemologically independent. Since HESPERUS and
PHOSPHORUS are different universals, the belief that a given relative
particular exemplifies HESPERUS is not epistemologically inconsistent
with a failure to believe that the same relative particular exemplifies
PHOSPHORUS. (86) and (89) are, moreover, each independent of either of
the pair (87, 90) (and conversely). For, (86, 89) assert relations of
relative particulars and universals, while (87, 90) assert relations
of universals and universals.

(v) (87) asserts the inclusion of HESPERUS in PHOSPHORUS, and
(90) the inclusion of PHOSPHORUS in HESPERUS. Each of these properties
is of cardinality 1. A belief in one of the inclusions unaccompanied
by a belief in the other would accordingly constitute epistemological
inconsistency.

(vi) Belief in the identity of two things is never solely a belief in the self-relatedness of a single aspect. It involves also a
joining together of different aspects. But phosphorus and hesperus
are not different apsects of the same particular. They are not only
identical; they are also the same.

How might the Greeks, while thinking about Hesperus and
Phosphorus, have failed--without epistemological prejudice--to realize
that Hesperus and Phosphorus were one and the same? Suppose them to
have thought:

116

95) Hesperus is̄ Hesperus.

96) Phosphorus is̄ Phosphorus.

In so thinking, they would have thought:

97) hesperus is HESPERUS

98) HESPERUS IS HESPERUS

99) phosphorus is PHOSPHORUS

100) PHOSPHORUS IS PHOSPHORUS

In thinking (97) they would have grasped Hesperus as Hesperus, for to grasp the connection between a relative particular and the property of being a specific particular is to grasp that the relative particular and property are aspects of the particular in question. Likewise, in thinking (99) they would have grasped Phosphorus as Phosphorus. But no number of such graspings of the self-identities of Hesperus and Phosphorus would ever have alone sufficed to lead to the conclusion that Hesperus and Phosphorus were one and the same. For the identity of Hesperus and Phosphorus involves the universals HESPERUS and PHOSPHORUS, whose interconnection is involved in the identity of neither Hesperus nor Phosphorus alone. The identity of two things thus involves a difference which the identity of one does not: the interconnection of universals which are relatively identical rather than absolutely so, because they are different aspects of the same thing.

What then is the basis of the discernibility of Hesperus and Phosphorus? Quite simply the fact that Leibniz notwithstanding, Hesperus and Phosphorus are identical yet different.

The chief contemporary account of singular identity-statements is that of Saul Kripke. In Naming and Necessity and other writings, Kripke develops an anti-Frege-Russell account of identity-statements

117

which many philosophers now accept. By way of concluding my account of the identity-relation, a brief commentary on Kripke's theory is thus appropriate.[95]

A Kripkean account of the difference between necessary and contingent identity-statements relies crucially upon the notion <u>rigid designator</u>. A <u>rigid designator</u> is a term which designates the same thing in every possible world in which that thing exists, and designates nothing in other possible worlds. A <u>non-rigid</u> designator designates different things in different worlds. The identity-statement "Hesperus is Phosphorus" is thus necessary, a Kripkean would say, because "Hesperus" and "Phosphorus" are rigid designators, while "Scott is the author of <u>Waverley</u>" is contingent because "the author of <u>Waverley</u>" is a non-rigid designator.

The chief defect of the Kripkean account is that it does nothing to explain what is really at stake in the foregoing identity-statements: the <u>essential</u> identity of Hesperus and Phosphorus, as contrasted with the <u>accidental</u> identity of Scott and the author of <u>Waverley</u>. About these <u>facts</u>, which are surely the <u>de re</u> basis of the necessary character of "Hesperus is Phosphorus" and the contingent character of "Scott is the author of <u>Waverley</u>", the Kripkean account has nothing to say. For if Hesperus and Phosphorus are <u>essentially</u> identical, as they most assuredly are, the <u>explanation</u> for this must reside in something <u>about</u> Hesperus and Phosphorus; and this can certainly not be that the <u>names</u> "Hesperus" and "Phosphorus" are associated with the same constant function! For surely, Hesperus would have been Phosphorus, even had "Hesperus" and "Phosphorus" never existed; and surely, Scott is only contingently the author of _Waverley_, no matter how we might choose to refer to him.

To be fair to Kripke, the Kripkean account does no more or less than its author judges proper, where the topic of contingent identity is concerned. For Kripke does not believe in _de re_ contingent identity. Thus, the thesis that identical objects are necessarily identical is, according to Kripke, a "self-evident" thesis of philosophical logic,[96] and its companion doctrine, the Leibnizian principle that such objects are indiscernible, is "as self-evident as the law of contradiction."[97] So for Kripke as well as for Russell and Frege, identity is a strictly internal relation.

Kripke thus reduces the question of whether an identity-statement is necessary or contingent to the question of whether its designators are rigid or non-rigid. The necessity or contingency of identity-statements is thus rooted not in the nature of things, but only in the way they are designated. But to take the position that Kripke does is to stand explanation on its head. For what could possibly account for the fact that "the author of _Waverley_" is a non-rigid designator other than the fact that the relative particular the author of waverley exemplifies the universal THE AUTHOR OF WAVERLEY, contingently and not necessarily? And what could possibly account for the fact that "Scott" is a rigid designator other than the fact that scott exemplifies SCOTT necessarily? Thus, the nature of a thing's identity is a ground, and not a consequence of rigid and non-rigid designation.

Unlike Frege, Russell and Kripke, I have thus aimed to make the nature of the identity-relation the basis for my account of identity-statements, and the nature of the particular the basis for my account of the identity-relation. Moreover, unlike Frege, Russell and Kripke, I have posited a particular which is two-sided and multi-faceted, a unity of the individual and the universal, and thus itself an exemplar of identity-in-difference.[98] Unlike the (implicitly) undifferentiated[99] particular of Frege, Russell and Kripke, the particular which I posit thus has a nature which allows it to enter into a rich variety of identity-relations. About each of these relations, the following may be said.

The identity-relation is a relation which, in relating a particular to itself, relates the particular to each of its aspects, and each of its aspects to the others. A particular's identity thus dwells in the unity of its aspects. Accordingly, whether its identity is necessary or contingent is a question of whether that unity can be undone.

[1]Particular will be understood as referring to an individual object, or the category of such objects, depending upon the context in which it occurs. Individual and universal will respectively be understood to represent the thatness and whatness of an individual object, or to the categories thereof, again depending on context.

[2]We would also be unable to reflect the nonconventional nature of the existence of Pegasus, in the unlikely event that Pegasus did exist. Thus, suppose that the sense of "Pegasus exists" is that Pegasus exemplifies the property expressed by "exists". Then the truth of this proposition would be guaranteed--unless we were willing to admit the possibility of non-existent objects--by a linguistic fact: the fact that "Pegasus" is a name, which it would not be if it did not name something.

[3]As Smullyan notes (cf. "Modality and Descriptions," p. 35, ff.), however, a sentence such as "Necessarily, the number of planets is nine" can also be construed as true. In 2.5 I will examine the factors which determine the truth or falsity of such a sentence.

[4]There is some disagreement as to the details of a Fregean account of negative existentials. If "exists" is taken to induce an oblique context (cf. Linsky '77, p. 38), semantical reconstruction will be primarily involved, as "Pegasus" will then denote its ordinary "sense". On the other hand, if "exists" is taken to express a second-level property of concepts, rather than a first-level concept of individuals (cf. Munitz '74, p. 75 ff.), syntactical reconstruction will be primarily involved. In either case, however, the particular is left out of account as the ontological subject of existence.

[5]Cf. Wilson (1980), p. 237.

[6]The expression ",XAWX" differs from ",xAWx" in that it signifies the attribute of being the author of Waverley rather than the individual (if any) which exemplifies that attribute.

[7]Thus, whereas (6, 8) assert a relation between a definite particular and the property of mortality, (7, 9) assert a relation between the totality of individuals and the property of mortality, a relation which holds just in case only one of those individuals has the property in question. Yet (7, 9) are no more about the totality than they are about any individual member, since the totality qua totality is not identified as a term of the relation asserted.

[8]Cf. Russell (1903), p. 47.

[9]In his book The Problems of Philosophy (1912), Russell takes a universal to be "anything which may be shared by many particulars..." (p. 93).

[10] In <u>PM</u>, the question does not arise whether phrases such as "a so-and-so" and "the so-and-so" function as logical subjects. For, the proposition of <u>PM</u> is an <u>extra</u>-linguistic entity, whose constituents are not its logically significant words and phrases but the entities which these words and phrases signify. At this stage in Russell's thought, there is thus no distinction between the <u>logical</u> subject of a proposition and its <u>ontological</u> subject, the thing whose properties and relations determine its truth.

[11] The distinction between "Socrates", which indicates a thing directly--and "the author of <u>Waverley</u>", which indicates a thing indirectly, by means of a denoting concept--is very much akin to Frege's distinction between the "sense" of an expression and its "reference". For the Russell of <u>PM</u>, as for Frege, it is thus the denoting concept (a "sense"), and not the thing which it deontes (the "reference"), that constitutes the <u>meaning</u> of a complex proper name. Whether or not there is a thing for the concept indicated by (e.g.) "the author of <u>Waverley</u>" to denote, thus has no bearing on the content of "The author of <u>Waverley</u> is mortal". Again, for Russell as for Frege, such a proposition is not <u>about</u> the denoting concept (the "sense") indicated by its subject term, although that denoting concept <u>is</u> one of its constituents. Instead it is about the <u>thing</u> (the "reference") that the concept denotes, the (onto)logical subject of the proposition. But Russell, unlike Frege, denies to ordinary proper names the mediated reference which he attributes to complex singular terms. In the case of "Socrates", there is thus no question of a denoting concept (a "sense") as distinct from a thing (a "reference") that a denoting concept might denote. Hence there is no distinction between what "Socrates" <u>means</u> in "Socrates is mortal" and what "Socrates is mortal" is <u>about</u>. For the <u>meaning</u> of "Socrates" (its "sense") is not given by a denoting concept separate from and prior to the thing it denotes (its "reference"). It is instead wholly determined by the individual thing which <u>"Socrates"</u> signifies (its "reference"), which is both what "Socrates" <u>means</u> in "Socrates is mortal", and what "Socrates is mortal" is <u>about</u>.

[12] Cf. Russell (1903), p. 53.

[13] Ibid., p. 62.

[14] The difference between the propositions expressed by (1) "The author of Waverley is mortal", and (II) "Scott is mortal", as these involve "the author of <u>Waverley</u>" and "Scott", can be illustrated as in the following diagrams:

(I') "the author of <u>Waverley</u>" → indicates → the denoting concept 'the author of <u>Waverley</u>'
↓
denotes
↓
the object
Scott

(II') "Scott" → indicates → the object Scott

122

Now, the proposition expressed by (I) has 'the author of <u>Waverley</u>', but not Scott, as one of its constituents, or ontological parts. On the assumption that the meaning of "The author of <u>Waverley</u> is mortal" is a function of its constituents (<u>not</u> the <u>meaning</u> of its constituents-- recall, a proposition is an <u>extra</u>-linguistic entity, whose constituents are objects and concepts), it is the denoting concept 'the author of <u>Waverley</u>' which enters into the meaning in question, and not Scott, the object denoted by that concept. On the other hand, the proposition expressed by (I) is not <u>about</u> the denoting concept 'the author of <u>Waverley</u>', but instead about Scott, the single, definite object denoted by that concept. Scott, and not 'the author of <u>Waverley</u>', is thus the (onto)logical subject of the proposition in question.

By contrast, in the proposition expressed by (II), the object Scott has a double function. In addition to being an (onto)logical subject, Scott is also a <u>constituent</u> of this proposition. Scott, the object, thus also enters into the meaning of (II), which it does not in (I), where the bearer of meaning is the denoting concept 'the author of <u>Waverley</u>'.

[15] Cf. Whitehead and Russell (1910), p. 66.

[16] Cf. Russell (1905), p. 51.

[17] Cf. Russell (1903), p. x.

[18] Cf. Russell (1918), p. 253.

[19] Ibid., p. 185.

[20] Ibid., p. 248.

[21] Ibid., p. 252.

[22] Ibid., p. 253.

[23] Cf. Russell (1959), p. 151.

[24] Cf. Russell (1919), p. 286.

[25] Cf. Russell (1918), p. 197.

[26] Ibid., p. 192.

[27] Cf. Russell (1914), p. 47.

[28] Cf. Russell (1918), p. 198.

[29] Cf. Russell (1914), p. 48.

[30] Cf. Russell (1919), p. 289.

[31]Cf. Russell (1918), p. 237.

[32]Cf. Stebbing, p. 144.

[33]Ibid., p. 43.

[34]Cf. Russell (1919), p. 286.

[35]Cf. Russell (1918), p. 238.

[36]At this point, one of the following objections might be raised to my contention that a monadic general fact can be derived from a monadic particular fact by substitution--and hence that a monadic general fact, and the proposition which describes it, have subject-predicate form:

> "The form of the fact that all men are mortal is different from the form of the fact that Socrates is mortal, in that the former involves a universal quantifier and a variable, whereas the latter does not. Therefore, one form cannot be derived from the other by substitution."

> "You are forgetting that sentences expressing general facts contain quantifiers."

The first objection prejudges the main ontological point at issue: whether an attribute of a particular functions as the ontological subject of a general fact, in the same way that a particular functions as the ontological subject of a particular fact. If it does function in this way, then in the light of the notion that two facts "...have the same form when they differ only as regards their constituents", it is difficult to see what basis there could be for the claim that a monadic general fact, but not a monadic particular fact, involves a universal quantifier and a variable. The second objection amounts to a repetition of what Frege and Russell teach: that general propositions, or sentences, contain quantifiers. In prejudging the correctness of the Frege-Russell tradition in this regard, it either sidesteps or begs the ontological questions which are here at stake.

[37]Cf. Russell (1959), p. 66.

[38]Cf. Stebbing, p. 50, n. 2.

[39]Cf. Russell (1918), p. 199.

[40]Ibid., p. 206.

[41]Ibid.

[42]Ibid., p. 201.

[43]Cf. Russell (1924), pp. 337-8.

[44] Cf. Russell (1918), p. 199.

[45] Cf. Veatch (1971), p. 108.

[46] Cf. Fitch (1950), p. 378.

[47] Fitch regards as misguided attempts by "past writers" (he gives no references) to treat attribution (our exemplification) as some sort of "partial identity". According to Fitch, such attempts amount to "trying to make one relation, identity, perform to some extent the function of another and wholly different relation, attribution." (p. 378) As we will see in 2.9, however, exemplification and inclusion are not related to the identity-relation, as Fitch would have us believe, as two distinct things to a third. Instead, exemplification and attribution are related to the identity-relation as aspects of a thing to the thing they are aspects of.

[48] "ALL MEN are mortal" is derived from "All men are mortal" by the process of attributivization. The motivation for this transformation is Russell's contention that such a sentence expresses a general, not a particular proposition.

[49] A property is _internal_ to a particular just in case it is an essential part of what the particular is:

(i) INT(f, x) $\leftrightarrow$ Nec(x=x $\longrightarrow$ f(x))

Having two legs is thus internal to a cyclist but not to a mathematician, for the cyclist could not remain a cyclist after losing a leg, but the mathematician could, in similar circumstances, remain a mathematician.

A property is _necessarily internal_ to a particular just in case it is internal to the particular, and the particular is what it is _necessarily_:

(ii) Nec(INT(f, x)) $\leftrightarrow$ Nec(x=x $\longrightarrow$ f(x)). Nec(x=x)

Having two legs is thus internal to a cyclist, but it is not _necessarily_ internal, for a cyclist is a cyclist only contingently. Similarly, being an odd number is a property which is internal to the number of planets, for the number of planets could not be what it is without being an odd number. But, being an odd number is not a property which is _necessarily_ internal to the number of planets, since the number of planets is what it is _contingently_ and _not_ _necessarily_. In contrast, being the smallest even prime is a property which is necessarily internal to the positive square root of four, which is what it is _necessarily_. Whether a property is _necessarily_ internal (external) to a particular is thus determined by whether the particular is necessarily self-identical. The basis for a distinction between necessary and contingent self-identity will be presented in section _2.7_.

[50]Of (23) there is the following proof:

1) Nec(x=x) . Pos Λf(x=x . ~f(x))   Assume
2) ~~Show--~Pos-Vf(Nec(x=x----→--f(x)))~~   Show
3) Pos Vf(Nec(x=x --→ f(x))   Assume
4) Nec(x=x)   1
5) Pos Vf(Nec(f(x)))   3, 4
6) Pos Λf~(f(x))   1
7) ~Pos Vf(Nec(f(x)))   6
8) ~Pos Vf(Nec(x=x --→ f(x))   3, 5, 7
9) Nec(x=x) . Pos Λf(x=x . ~f(x)) --→
     ~Pos Vf(Nec(x=x --→ f(x)))   1, 2

1) Nec(x=x) . ~Pos Vf(Nec(x=x --→ f(x)))   Assume
2) ~~Show--Pos-Λf(x=x-.--~f(x))--~~
3) ~Pos Λf(x=x . ~f(x))   Assume
4) Nec Vf~(x=x . ~f(x))   3
5) Nec Vf(x=x --→ f(x))   4
6) ~Nec Vf(x=x --→ f(x))   1
7) Pos Λf(x=x . ~f(x))   3, 5, 6
8) Nec(x=x) . ~Pos Vf(Nec(x=x --→ f(x))) --→
     Pos Λf(x=x . ~f(x))   1, 2

[51](25) follows from (24) by virtue of the theorem

$$[\sim Nec(p \rightarrow q) . Nec\ p] \longrightarrow \sim Nec\ q$$

[52]Cf. Russell (1919), p. 203.

[53]According to thesis (A)(p. 44), (1) expresses not a particular but a general proposition. We will ultimately see that (1), and singular sentences generally, express propositions that are both particular and general.

[54]When "not" is taken as a predicate-forming operator:

PEGASUS not-exists

"Pegasus does not exist" will count as false.

[55]Why, it might be asked, can "exists" not be taken as "exists$_1$", so that we have:

(i) The property of being Pegasus exists$_1$

126

In contrast to "Pegasus", which belongs to the category of particular-denoting terms, "the property of being Pegasus" belongs to the category of property-of-particular denoting terms. The consequences of this difference emerge upon consideration of

(i')   the property of being pegasus exists$_1$

and

(i'')   THE PROPERTY OF BEING PEGASUS exists$_1$,

each of which captures one term of the ambiguity inherent in (i).

In (i') the property of being Pegasus, a property of particulars, is asserted to <u>exemplify</u> existence$_1$, which is also a property of particulars. But the former cannot possibly exemplify the latter: particulars exemplify properties of particulars, properties of particulars do not. In (ii') the property of being the property of being Pegasus, a property of properties of particulars, is asserted to be <u>included</u> in existence$_1$, a property of particulars. But the former cannot possibly be included in the latter: properties of particulars are included in properties of particulars, properties of properties of particulars are not.

This is why it is not possible to construe "exists" in (i) as "exists$_1$".

[56] An analysis of <u>necessary</u> inclusion is presented on p. (92).

[57] "P" and "PEGASUS" signify the same property, the property of being Pegasus. However, "P" denotes this property as a predicate, and "PEGASUS" denotes this property as a subject.

[58] I will maintain here, against Kripke, that there is a category of contingent identity. Thus, Scott and the author of <u>Waverley</u> are contingently identical, unlike Hesperus and Phosphorus, which are necessarily identical. With the help of the notions <u>internal</u> and <u>necessarily</u> <u>internal</u> property (cf. note 49), let us see why this is so.

(i) Being Scott is internal to the author of <u>Waverley</u>, since it is not possible for the author of <u>Waverley</u> to be the author of <u>Waverley</u> without being Scott. Being Scott is not <u>necessarily</u> internal to the author of <u>Waverley</u> however, since the author of <u>Waverley</u> is only contingently the author of <u>Waverley</u>.

(ii) Being the author of <u>Waverley</u> is neither internal nor necessarily internal to Scott, since it is possible for Scott to be Scott without being the author of <u>Waverley</u>.

Let us now say that particulars <u>x</u> and <u>y</u> are <u>necessarily</u> identical just in case being <u>x</u> is necessarily internal to <u>y</u>, and being <u>y</u> is necessarily internal to <u>x</u>. Particulars <u>x</u> and <u>y</u> will then be

contingently identical if they are identical but not necessarily
identical. Finally, particulars x and y will be identical if being y
is one of x's properties, and conversely. By the foregoing criteria,
Scott and the author of Waverley are contingently identical. We will
now see that Hesperus and Phosphorus are necessarily identical.

(iii) Being Phosphorus is internal to Hesperus, since it is not
possible for Hesperus to be Hesperus without also being Phosphorus.
Being Phosphorus is necessarily internal to Hesperus moreover, for
Hesperus is necessarily Hesperus.

The same principles apply, mutandis mutandum, to Phosphorus and
being Hesperus. Hesperus and Phosphorus are thus necessarily identical.

The preceding analysis presupposes a distinction between
necessary and contingent self-identity. The basis for such a distinction is presented in section 2.7.

[59] "S" and "SCOTT" signify the same property, as do "AW" and "THE
AUTHOR OF WAVERLEY". However, "S" and "AW" denote these properties as
predicates, while "SCOTT" and "THE AUTHOR OF WAVERLEY" denote them as
subjects.

[60] Cf. Russell (1959), p. 85.

[61] Cf. Alston, p. 234.

[62] As we will see in 2.7, such sentences also convey particular
propositions.

[63] In the example, "necessarily" occurs as a proposition-forming
operator.

[64] Cf. 2.51 and notes 53 and 54.

[65] Cf. Russell (1918), p. 252.

[66] By a connotative singular term, I mean any expression which (i)
denotes a particular object or person, if it denotes; and, (ii) denotes
what it denotes by virtue of that thing's possessing an attribute or
attributes which the term connotes. Examples of such terms are "John's
brother", "the present King of France", "this book", etc.

[67] Cf. Ayer, p. 37.

[68] In PLA, Russell says (p. 232):

"When you take any propositional function and assert...
that it is sometimes true, that gives you the fundamental
meaning of existence. You may express it by saying that
there is at least one value of x for which that propositional
function is true. Take 'x is a man', there is at least one

value of $\underline{x}$ for which this is true. That is what one means by saying that...'Men exist'."

Thus, for Russell "Men exist" must be construed as

(i) Men exist$_2$,

where what is asserted is that the property of being a man, a property of particulars, exemplifies existence$_2$, a property of properties of particulars. We have already seen that for such a property to exemplify existence$_2$, some property of particulars must have it. So for the property of being a man to exist$_2$, something must exemplify the property of being a man. This is the sense of Russell's passage.

But "Men exist" can also be construed as

(ii) Men exist$_1$.

What (ii) asserts is that the property of being a man is included in existence$_1$, a property of particulars. The difference between (i) and (ii) is apparent. (i) will be true as long as there are men. (ii) will be true as long as nothing which is a man fails to exist$_1$. The difference between the interpretations in question is more apparent in the case of "Dragons exist". Construed as

(iii) Dragons exist$_2$,

this sentence is arguably true, on the assumption that Faffner is indeed a dragon. However, construed as

(iv) Dragons exist$_1$,

this sentence is undeniably false, since whatever Faffner's other properties may be, existence$_1$ is not among them.

[69] For the word "name" may hereinafter be substituted the phrase "genuine proper name", salva significatum.

[70] Exemplification and inclusion are not introduced here as a means of eliminating the predication relation, as Russell introduces classes of exemplification relations as a means of eliminating the inclusion relation. Exemplification and inclusion instead pose themselves as distinct forms of a predication relation whose nature is bound up in the nature of its terms.

[71] The derivation of line (8) from lines (1, 5) presupposes the validity of the conditional

(i) Nec $\Lambda x(F(x)) \dashrightarrow \Lambda x(Nec(F(x)))$.

Suppose that (i) is not valid. Then (ii) is consistent.

(ii)   Nex Λx(F(x)) . ~Λx(Nec(F(x)))

But from "~Λx(Nec(F(x)))", it follows that:

(iii)   Vx(~Nec(F(x)))

(iv)   Vx(Pos(~F(x)))

(v)   Pos(Vx(~F(x)))

(vi)   ~Nec~Vx(~F(x))

(vii)   ~Nec Λx(F(x))

But from (vii) and (ii) we have

(viii)   ~Nec Λx(F(x)) . Nec Λx(F(x)).

Thus, (ii) is inconsistent, and (i) is valid.

[72] Cf. Russell (1905), p. 48.

[73] Cf. Strawson (1950), p. 155.

[74] Ibid.

[75] Ibid., p. 156.

[76] Ibid.

[77] Ibid., p. 157.

[78] Cf. Strawson (1960), p. 188.

[79] The assertoric function of a subject-predicate sentence, _qua_ vehicle of a _general_ proposition is, however, subject to the restriction that its logical subject denote a _property_.

[80] A particular-denoting singular term "φ" denotes a particular _x_, just in case _x_ uniquely has _X_, where _X_ is the property denoted by the corresponding property-denoting singular term "$\overset{\sim}{\Phi}$".

[81] Symbolically, we thus have:

(i)   Nec(x ∈ Y ←→ ~Pos Vz(z=x . ~(z ∈ Y))

(ii)   Nec(X ⊆ Y ←→ ~Pos Vz(z ∈ X . ~(z ∈ Y))

where lower-range variables range over particulars, upper-case variables range over properties, and "∈" and "⊆" signify, respectively, the exemplification and inclusion relations.

[82]The notion of "rigid" designation was introduced by Kripke as a way of distinguishing terms which denote the same thing in each "possible world" that it exists (rigid designators) from terms which designate different things in different worlds (non-rigid designators). The possibility of Mary's husband not being Mary's husband is thus related to the fact that "Mary's husband" is a non-rigid designator, whose denotation can vary from world to world. On my analysis, the fact that "Mary's husband" is a non-rigid designator has the same source as the possibility of Mary's husband not being Mary's husband: the contingent self-identity of Mary's husband.

[83]Cf. Plantinga (1974), p. 70.

[84]Assume that: (i) the property of being the number of planets exists$_2$. Then, for exactly one number x, x has this property. But then, (i) the subject$_0$ exists$_1$, since x is the subject$_0$. Furthermore, (iii) the subject$_0$ exemplifies the predicate$_0$, since the predicate$_0$ is the property of being the number of planets.

Assume that: (i) the subject$_0$ exists$_1$. Then, for exactly one number x, x has the property of being the number of planets. Hence, (ii) the predicate$_0$ exists$_2$, and (iii) the subject$_0$ exemplifies the predicate$_0$,

Assume that: (iii) the subject$_0$ exemplifies the predicate$_0$. Then, (i) the subject$_0$ exists$_1$, and therefore, as shown above, (ii) the predicate$_0$ exists$_2$.

[85]The general necessity proposition (59), of course, fails to correspond to a fact, while its particular counterpart (58) does correspond to a fact. What is at issue here is a demonstration that (59, 58) are ontologically independent, solely on the basis of what it is for a property X to be necessarily included in a property Y, or for a particular x to exemplify a property Y necessarily.

[86]Cf. Dummett (1973), p. 544. Quoted in Miller (1975), p. 348.

[87]Marcus states this as: "If $a = b$ then every property of a is a property of b." (Marcus, 1975, p. 32).

[88]Cf. p. 59.

[89]That particulars cannot be described is a consequence of the fact that they are what they are by not being anything (cf. p. 62). That they cannot be named follows as a consequence of the argument from "exists" (cf. pp. 76 - 79).

[90]Cf. Allaire (1963), p. 14.

[91]A formal identity-statement is one whose terms are the same. A material identity statement is one whose terms are different.

[92]I will follow Baylis (1965), in characterizing as a universal "any quality, property, or relation of which we can conceive". (p. 16)

[93]Paul Schachter pointed out to me that identity-statements required interpretations for the case where both terms designated relative particulars. Out of my subsequent consternation the notion "relative particular" was born.

[94]On the side leading from the _individual_ (the "relative particular") to the universal, formal identity-statements are thus _not_ truisms; the discovery that Abbie Hoffman was Abbie Hoffman would not have been an uneventful one for a government agent who made it.

[95]I here borrow liberally from Greenberg (1981).

[96]Cf. Kripke (1981), p. 4.

[97]Ibid., p. 3.

[98]The individual and the universal are _identical_ because they are interconnected aspects of a self-same unity (the particular). They are _different_, in the _Hegelian_ sense, because each negates (limits, _determines_) the other. Thus, to be Scott is to be a particular. But it is not to be an _indeterminate_ particular. It is to be some _specific_ particular. The property of _being_ _Scott_ (rather than Jones, or Cicero, or Gargantua) thus _negates_ the relative particular scott which exemplifies it, making it something _specific_, the particular Scott. But the individual also negates (limits, determines) the universal. For the property of being Scott, although a universal, is _particularized_ by being a property _of_ Scott (rather than _of_ Jones, Cicero, or Gargantua). This property thus derives its individual character--that which differentiates it from _other_ instances of the same universal--only in, and through, its connection with the relative particular scott. The universal thus negates the individual, and the individual negates the universal. Their union within the particular thus constitutes an example of identity-in-difference.

A more familiar example, to linguists, of identity-in-difference would be the relation between the phonetic and the phonological content of the phoneme. These are complementary sides of the phoneme, in that neither could exist without the other. That is, there is no such thing as a phoneme with no extrinsic phonetic content, nor is there any such thing as a phoneme with no structural relations to the phonological system of a language. Moreover, the phonetic and phonological sides of the phoneme mutually _negate_ (determine, limit) one another. Thus, its phonological side (which rules it undergoes, how it undergoes them, etc.) is determined by its intrinsic phonetic content. But the phonetic content is also determined by which rules it undergoes, how it undergoes them, etc. The union within the phoneme of an intrinsic phonetic content and a systemic phonological content thus constitutes an example of identity-in-difference.

Undifferentiated in the sense that this unity is not understood as a unity of opposites, of the individual and the universal. Failure to analyze the particular as a unity of the individual and the universal makes it impossible to analyze the relations into which particulars enter qua particulars, which are logical and epistemological in character. Thus, for example, the persistent puzzlement over the nature of the identity-relation, which does obtain only between a particular and itself, but not the undifferentiated--and undifferentiable--particular of Frege, Russell and Kripke.

To draw a historical parallel. Suppose Marx had perceived the commodity as undifferentiated, and not as the unity of use-value and exchange-value. Would it then have been possible to give a correct account of the relations which commodities, and their owners, enter into?

Or, suppose that Chomsky and Halle had not perceived the phoneme as both concrete and relational in nature. Would they then have been able to write SPE?

BIBLIOGRAPHY

Ackermann, Diana (1976) "Plantinga, Proper Names, and Propositions,"
    Philosophical Studies 30 (1976), pp. 409-412.

Allaire, Edwin (1963) "Bare Particulars," in Nijhoff (1963),
    pp. 14-21.

Alston, W. (1967) "Meaning," in Edwards (1967), Vol. 5, pp. 233-240.

Anderson, A. R., Marcus and Martin (eds.) (1975) The Logical
    Enterprise. Yale U. Press.

Ayer, A. (1971) Russell and Moore: The Analytical Heritage. London,
    MacMillan.

Bahm, A. (1972) Metaphysics. New York, Harper and Row.

Baylis, Charles A. (ed.) (1965) Metaphysics. Collier-MacMillan.

Behmann, Heinrich (1963) "Three Paradoxical Aspects of Identity,"
    Ratio 5, pp. 113-139, Dec. '63.

Bostock, David (1977) "Kripke on Identity and Necessity," Philo-
    sophical Quarterly, Vol. 27, 1977, pp. 313-324.

Burge, Tyler (1977) "Belief De Re," Journal of Philosophy, Vol. 74,
    No. 6, pp. 338-362.

Butchvarov, P. (1979) "Identity," in French (1979), pp. 159-178.

Butler, R. J. (ed.) (1956) Analytical Philosophy. Second Series,
    Oxford, Basil Blackwell.

Cargile, James (1970) "Davidson's Notion of Logical Form," Inquiry 13,
    pp. 129-139, Summer 1970.

Cartwright, Richard (1971) "Identity and Substitutivity," in Munitz
    (ed.) (1971), pp. 119-134.

Clack, Robert J. (1969) Bertrand Russell's Philosophy of Language,
    ed. Martinus Nijhoff, The Hague.

Copi, Irvine (1951) "Philosophy and Language," Review of Metaphysics,
    Vol. IV, No. 3, March 1951, pp. 427-437.

Donnellan, Keith (1966) "Reference and Definite Descriptions,"
    Philosophical Review, lxxv.

Edwards, P. (ed.) (1967) The Encyclopedia of Philosophy, Vol. 1-8.
    New York, MacMillan.

Fitch, Frederick (1950) "Actuality, Possibility, and Being," Review
    of Metaphysics, Vol. 3, March 1950, pp. 367-384.

Flew, Anthony (ed.) (1965) Logic and Language. Anchor Books, Doubleday.

French, P., Uehling, T., and Wettstein, H. (eds.) (1979) Contemporary
    Perspectives in The Philosophy of Language. Minnesota,
    University of Minnesota Press.

Fritz, Charles A. (1952) Bertrand Russell's Construction of the
    External World. Routledge, Kegal & Paul.

Geatch, P. T. (1970) "A Program for Syntax," reprinted in Logic and
    Philosophy for Linguists, ed. J. M. E. Moravcsik, The Hague,
    1974, pp. 238-250.

Godfrey-Smith, William (1976) "Names, Indices and Individuals,"
    Analysis, Vol. 37, No. 1, Oct. 1976.

Godfrey-Smith, William (1978) "Prior and Particulars," Philosophy,
    Vol. 53, No. 205, July 1978.

Gram, M. S. (1971) "Ontology and the Theory of Descriptions," in
    Klemke (ed.), pp. 118-143.

Greenberg, William J. (1980) "Identity," unpublished ms.

Greenberg, William J. (1976) "De Dicto and De Re Without Relative Scope,"
    Papers From the Twelfth Regional Meeting (Chicago Linguistic
    Society).

Hochberg, Herbert (1978) Thought, Fact, and Reference: The Origins and
    Ontology of Logical Atomism. University of Minnesota Press,
    Minneapolis.

Kalish, Donald (1952) "Logical Form," Mind LXI, pp. 56-71.

Kaplan, David (1966) "What is Russell's Theory of Descriptions?" in
    Pears (ed.) (1972), pp. 227-244.

Kielkopf, Charles (1977) "There is no Really Rigid Designation,"
    Nous 11, 1977, pp. 409-416.

Klemke, E. (ed.) (1971) Essays on Bertrand Russell. Chicago,
    University of Illinois Press.

Kripke, Saul (1976) "A Puzzle About Belief," in Margalit (ed.),
    pp. 239-283.

Kripke, Saul (1971) "Identity and Necessity," in Munitz (ed.) (1971),
    pp. 135-164.

Kripke, Saul (1972) <u>Naming and Necessity</u>. Harvard U. Press, Cambridge, Massachusetts. 1981.

Lenin, V. (1915) "On the Question of Dialectics," in <u>The Collected Works of V. I. Lenin</u> (1972), Progress Publishers, Moscow, Vol. 38, pp. 355-363.

Linsky, Leonard (1977) <u>Names and Descriptions</u>. Univ. of Chicago Press, Chicago.

Linsky, L. (ed.) (1971) <u>Reference and Modality</u>. London, Oxford University Press.

Linsky, L. (1969) "Reference, Essentialism, and Modality," in Linsky (ed.) (1971), pp. 89-100.

Lockwood, Michael (1971) "Identity and Reference," in Munitz (ed.) (1971), pp. 199-212.

Lockwood, Michael (1975) "On Predicating Proper Names," <u>Philosophical Review</u> 84, October 1975, pp. 471-498.

Marcus, Ruth Barcan (1975) "Does the Principle of Substitutivity Rest on a Mistake?" in Anderson, A. R. et. al. (eds.) (1975), pp. 31-38.

Margalit, A. (ed.) (1976) <u>Meaning and Use</u>. Dordrecht, D. Reidel.

Marsh, R. (ed.) (1971) <u>Logic and Knowledge</u>. New York, Allen and Unwin.

Miller, Barry (1975) "In Defence of the Predicate Exists," <u>Mind</u> (1975), series 2, Vol. 84, No. 335, pp. 338-354.

Moore, G. E. (1936) "Is Existence a Predicate?" in Flew (ed.) (1965), pp. 299-311.

Munitz, Milton K. (1974) <u>Existence and Logic</u>. New York University Press.

Munitz, Milton (ed.) (1971) <u>Identity and Individuation</u>. New York University Press, New York.

Mijhoff, Martinus (ed.) (1963) <u>Essays in Ontology</u>. Iowa Publications in Philosophy, Vol. 1, Iowa City.

Orenstein, Alex (1975) "Strawson, Frege and Hilbert on Meaning and Definite Descriptions," <u>Ratio</u>, Vol. 17, No. 1, June 1975, pp. 91-98.

Partee, Barbara (1975) "Montague and Transformational Grammar," <u>Linguistic Inquiry</u>, Vol. VI, Number 2, pp. 203-300.

Pears, D. F. (ed.) (1972) Bertrand Russell: A Collection of Critical Essays. Anchor Books, Doubleday.

Pears, D. F. (1967) Bertrand Russell and the British Tradition in Philosophy. Random House, New York.

Pears, D. F. (1963) "Is Existence a Predicate?" in Strawson (ed.) (1967), pp. 97-102.

Peterson, John (1976) Realism and Logical Atomism. The University of Alabama Press.

Peterson, John (1976) "Realism, Propositions, and Professor Veatch," New Scholasticism, Vol. L, No. 4, pp. 464-480.

Plantinga, A. (1978) "The Boethian Compromise," American Philosophical Quarterly, Vol. 15, No. 2, April 1978, pp. 129-138.

Plantinga, A. (1970) The Nature of Necessity. Clarendon Press, Oxford.

Prior, A. N. (1971) Objects of Thought. Oxford University Press.

Prior, A. N. (1976) The Doctrine of Propositions and Terms. University of Massachusetts Amherst Press.

Quine, W. (1960) Word and Object. Cambridge, MIT Press.

Rundle, B. (1956) "Modality and Quantification," in Analytical Philosophy, R. J. Butler (ed.), pp. 27-39.

Russell, B. (1903) The Principles of Mathematics. New York,. W. W. Morton and Company, 2nd edition.

Russell, B. (1905) "On Denoting," in Marsh (1971), pp. 41-56.

Russell, B. (1910) Principia Mathematica (to #56). With A. N. Whitehead. New York, Cambridge University Press.

Russell, B. (1912) The Problems of Philosophy. New York, Oxford University Press.

Russell, B. (1914) Our Knowledge of the External World. New York, The New American Library.

Russell, B. (1918) "The Philosophy of Logical Atomism," in Marsh, op. cit., pp. 178-281.

Russell, B. (1919) "On Propositions: What They Are and How They Mean," in March, op. cit., pp. 285-320.

Russell, B. (1924) "Logical Atomism," in Marsh, op. cit., pp. 323-343.

Russell, B. (1959) My Philosophical Development. London, Allen and Unwin.

Searle, John D. (1958) "Proper Names," in Strawson (ed.) (1967), pp. 89-96.

Searle, John R. (1979) "Referential and Attributive," The Monist, Vol. 62, 1979, pp. 191-208.

Shwayder, D. S. (1956) "=," Mind 65, pp. 16-37, January 1956.

Smith, Godfrey (1979) "Thoughts of Objects," The Monist, Vol. 62, pp. 223-235.

Smullyan, A. (1948) "Modality and Description," in Linsky (1971), pp. 35-43.

Stebbing, S. (1930) A Modern Introduction to Logic. London, Methuen & Co., 2nd edition.

Strawson, P. (1950) "On Referring," in Klemke (1971), pp. 147-172.

Strawson, P. F. (1960) Introduction to Logical Theory. London: Methuen & Co.

Strawson, P. F. (ed.) (1967) Philosophical Logic. Oxford Uniersity Press.

Stroll, A. (1967) "Identity," in Edwards (1967), Vol. 4, pp. 121-124.

Swindler, J. K. (1980) "Parmenides Paradox: Negative Reference and Negative Existentials," Journal of Metaphysics, Vol. XXXIII, June 1980, pp. 727-744.

Tichy, Pavel (1971) "An Approach to Intensional Analysis," Nous 5, September 1971, pp. 273-298.

Tichy, Pavel (1972) "Plantinga on Essence: A Few Questions," Philosophical Review, Vol. 81, January 1972, pp. 82-93.

Tichy, Pavel (1975) "What Do We Talk About?" Philosophy of Science 42, March 1975, pp. 80-93.

Urmson, J. O. (1956) Philosophical Analysis: Its Development Between the Two World Wars. Oxford University Press.

Veatch, Henry B. (1952) Intentional Logic: A Logic Based on Philosophical Realism. Yale University Press.

Veatch, Henry B. (1954) Realism and Nominalism Revisited. The
Aquinas Lecture, 1954. Marquette University Press, Milwaukee.

Veatch, Henry B. (1971) "The Philosophy of Logical Atomism: A Realism
Manqué", in Klemke (ed.), pp. 102-117.

Wells, Harry Kohlsaat (1950) Process and Unreality: A Criticism of
Method in Whitehead's Philosophy. King's Crown Press, Columbia
University, New York.

Wiggins, D. (1956) "Identity-Statements," in Analytical Philosophy,
R. J. Butler (ed.), pp. 40-71.

Wilson, W. Kent (1980) "Incomplete Symbols and Russell's Proof,"
Canadian Journal of Philosophy, Vol. X, No. 2, June 1980,
pp. 233-250.

www.ingramcontent.com/pod-product-compliance
Ingram Content Group UK Ltd.
Pitfield, Milton Keynes, MK11 3LW, UK
UKHW020416010325
455677UK00029B/908